Snapshots: Narratives and Interviews of Young Japanese Women

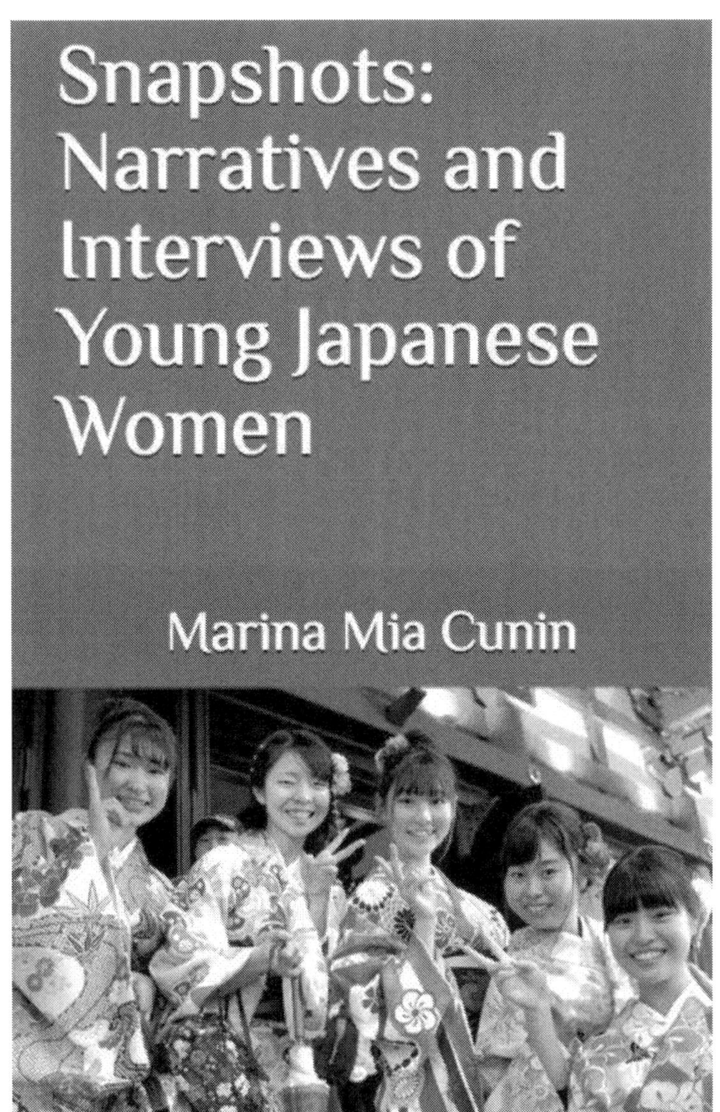

Fieldwork Publications

2014

First Published: 2014

Library of Congress Control Number: 9780990353409

ISBN: 978-0-9903534-0-9

Published by Fieldwork Publications

www.fieldworkpublications.com

Printed in the United States of America

To my mother Vashti Penelope

Table of Contents

Foreword i
Acknowledgments ii
Introduction 1
Chizuro 5
Junko 13
Akemi 21
Aiko 31
Haruko 39
Reiko 45
Asami 51
Aki 57
Yuri 73
Mami 81
Glossary 89
About the author 93

Foreword

Dr. Marina Mia Cunin has skillfully woven together the first-hand account of young Japanese women. These concise portraits are at once intensely personal, yet very revealing of the way wider issues of family, gender, sexuality, body image and mental health are played out in the specific context of Japan. A fascinating and truly gripping read.

Dr. Beverley Bishop, author *of Globalisation and Women in the Japanese Workforce* (2005) UK: RoutledgeCurzon

Acknowledgments

To all of the young women who took the time to share their experiences with me and whose words affected me on many levels, from positively influencing my teaching methods, to ensuring that I remained empathetic to the many ways in which young women experience their lives.

Thank you to John Clayton for all the preparation work we did together and to Vicki Zalascek for her editing skills.

Introduction

Throughout my transformative years in Japan, I was privileged to have several young women share their experiences with me. Between 2008 and 2012, I conducted semi-structured interviews in informal settings with twenty-three young women. The ten narratives and interviews presented here were selected out of the original twenty-three. They were chosen either based on their topics, or their representations of repetitive themes, such as anxieties about future full-time employment, family pressures, parental divorce, issues of sexuality, or mental health concerns.

The initial reference point for documenting my interest in young women's reflections came from asking for comments for one of my classes. I already had friendly relationships with several young women whom I met through past teaching assignments, women's groups, and religious organizations. Therefore, I asked whether they would be prepared to share some individual perspectives about their lives for my class on women's issues. They agreed and introduced me to other friends. This inadvertent snowball sampling resulted in me securing several thought-provoking short interviews on general attitudes to work, family, and relationships.

The interviews and classroom discussions that ensued were stimulating and challenging. Focusing on young women's reflections of their own experiences was one way to gain a deeper understanding behind the existing stereotypes of passive Japanese youth. It also highlighted how young women endeavored to negotiate their identities and situations from powerless social positions.

However, incorporating these interviews into more formal research raised several methodological and ethical issues for me. I needed to consider the power relationships that existed between the researcher and the researched given the importance of age and status in Japanese society. The Hawthorne effect was also applicable, as it proposed that the researched could alter how they recounted events and emotions due to their perceptions of the researcher being seen as a sympathetic interviewer. Issues of culture, cultural preconceptions, and language needed to be highlighted in the case of a non-Japanese woman interviewing Japanese women. Elements of language, meaning, and interpretation were further significant, as we communicated in Japanese, English, and a hybrid version of the two languages.

My attempts to explain and manage all these issues eventually ended my ideas for formal research. Nevertheless, I continued to share conversations with these young friends, meeting them in the relaxed settings of coffee shops, restaurants, and "Women's Night" at clubs and bars. The topics ranged from boring teachers, patronizing bosses, challenging families, problems with partners, girlfriends, and boyfriends, to trying to get a job interview and mental health issues. Three of the women presented here called me *Onee san* as a demonstration of our relationship, even though they were aware I was more their mothers' age.

There were several occasions when I returned to jotting down revealing comments and scenarios about their young lives, mindful of the words of Studs Terkel, an enduring hero of mine.

"I don't want anybody to be hurt by what I write... If I talk to somebody and she calls me afterwards and says, 'Please take out that bit about my husband drinking too much' - of course I take it out. It's none of my business." (Terkel, 2002[1])

---

[1] Burkeman, Oliver (Feb 28 2002) "Voice of America: Oliver Burkeman on Studs Terkel" Retrieved from

I always asked my friends' permission to use their words for any potential article. However, there were occasions when some refused, which was challenging as I felt their words and experiences would have created a deeper understanding of their situations. However, I respected their wishes. Those moments of inclusive or exclusive notetaking reaffirmed my awareness of the privilege of having young women share parts of their personal lives with me.

"Onee san, I forgot that's how we first met (laughing) *because you wanted to ask me about my views on life, my life. What happened to your research? We had Starbucks and conversation instead*." (Akemi)

In my final year in Japan ending in April 2012, I returned to document the reflections of these young women asking for more formal interviews using narrative interview techniques. In my data collection, I included summaries of settings in which we met over the years and notes of other individuals I met with them. I regained consent for the collected information but was still unclear about how to present this material. My main concern was that my methodology fell short of the rightful rigors of the academic research process.

"How about your research? I hope you can tell my story, maybe another girl has a story like mine." (Chizuro)

In 2013, women's realities crept to the forefront of contemporary Japanese society through Prime Minister Abe's employment policies focusing on women's participation. I wondered at the effect, if any, of these programs on the lives of my young friends. Working with John Clayton, a friend and colleague, I sent some of the interviews in fictionalized vignettes to him, not complete ethnographic fiction. He spearheaded an article, editing and re-

---

https://studs.uchicago.edu/voice-of-america-oliver-burkeman-on-studs-terkel/

writing them for journals. Although we were not successful in our publishing endeavors, one reviewer noted these women's stories needed to be heard.

Therefore, leaving behind the academic postulating and research formalities, I decided to present a sample of both the vignettes and original interviews. The narratives are not sophisticated pieces of literary fiction, but an attempt to creatively frame the women's actual words from their interviews.

Through their voices, these young women both confirm and challenge common assumptions about their generation while illustrating the social limitations on their lives due to their gender and age. And while some are presented here as fictional characters, their valid reflections shed light on Japanese society and the realities of daily life for young women in Japan.

Chizuro

"Ohayo!" sang out two high-pitched voices as twenty-year-old Chizuro sluggishly entered the English writing classroom. She knew the morning greeting was unlikely to be for her, so she didn't turn her head in the direction of her classmates sitting in the back row. She never sat there. That row was reserved for the bold and brazen girls with their rainbow-painted nails, and blond and orange locks; the girls who placed a mirror on their desk before their textbooks, and who blatantly ignored the teacher's numerous requests to put away all makeup, mirrors, and cellphones at the start of class.

Wearing the same clothes she wore two days ago; a long plaid shirt over slim black jeans purchased from *Uniqlo*, the renowned Japanese fashion chain; she had seen at least three other girls in the same shirt, and it was only 10.30 am. That was a good sign. She had chosen her outfit well if others were also wearing it.

She made her way to her usual seat in the far corner of the room, purposely away from the teacher's desk. From the front of the classroom, the seat was somewhat hidden, and unless the teacher decided to walk around the room or call her name to answer a question, it was a good place in which to be forgotten.

Her unsteady steps looked visually uncomfortable as her metallic blue high heels continued to clack noisily on the floor. She couldn't afford to buy shoes in her size of 23.0. Instead, like many other students she knew, she shopped at 'Seventeen', where she could buy two pairs of shoes for three thousand yen. The downside was that she had to buy a generic M-size pair, which left at least a finger-sized space between her heel and the back of the shoe. However, as long as the Seventeen purchases continued to deliver the desired response of "*kawaii!*" from her best friend, she was more than happy to continue with her version of being *Shinderera's* step-sister with small feet in large glass slippers.

Putting her oversized pink bag labeled, 'lesportssac', on top of the desk, she pulled out her phone; a miniature teddy bear dangled from it, along with three pink and red glitter-coated heart-shaped charms. Head down, her black hair, cut in a now-overgrown asymmetrical bob, covered half of her round make-up-free face, as she quickly texted Ayumi.

"I'm in class, where are you?"

"I'm coming," Ayumi responded.

Relief. The class would be bearable.

She had met Ayumi on the first day of their English communication class at the private women's college. They'd sat at the same desk and had to do the mandatory introductions.

"Hello, my name is Chizuro. I'm from Gifu, how about you?"

"Hello, my name is Ayumi. I'm from Gifu too."

"Oh really?"

"Yes."

The stilted and written conversation had been repeated in each one of their six English classes. But whenever the teacher was occupied with other students, they switched to speaking in Japanese, and that is how Chizuro discovered their commonalities. They each had a younger sibling, rarely saw their uncommunicative s*ararīmen* fathers, and felt pressured by the ambitious dreams of their mothers.

"Why did you come to this college?" Ayumi asked.

"My mother read about it and said if I graduate from here, I'll be able to speak English and work in the city for an international company."

"Yes, mine too, although my father thinks the school fees are too expensive. But my mother told him if I come here, I'll become a sophisticated office lady and get married to a manager."

Chizuro knew that the transformation from awkward, introverted teenagers into bilingual, delicate office flowers was next to impossible for both of them.

Now in the last semester of her two-year degree, she considered Ayumi her best friend, enough to copy homework from her, give her answers to test questions whenever possible, and share secrets of anxiety.

Seeing the overly happy foreign teacher enter the classroom triggered her usual response. Her stomach tightened at the thought that in the next seventy minutes, it was possible that the teacher would ask her a question and she would have to respond in English. When Ayumi was there, she could say her standard "I don't understand", but when she was on her own, no words came out. Still, the teacher always pushed her for a response despite receiving her blank stare.

"Foreign teachers are nice, but they don't understand Japanese students," Ayumi had once sighed.

Chizuro agreed, adding, "I don't know why we can't just watch foreign movies and listen to American music."

It wasn't that she didn't want to learn English. In high school, she'd harbored a dream that one day she would wake up magically fluent in

English, but now with one semester before graduation, reality had quickly erased such thoughts. Despite what this teacher and her mother had hoped for, she knew she wasn't going to need English in her future job, so why bother trying.

Reaching to the side of her head, she gently pulled on some of her hair. It was sparse in that section from where she had pulled it out completely, but it didn't show hidden behind her right ear.

"Aren't you afraid your hair won't grow back?" Ayumi asked.

"No. It will. I like to do it. It feels good. When the root comes free from the head, I feel happy. I know I'm crazy, right?" she laughed quietly. "But if I have a problem and I do this, then my problem feels less," enlightening her friend.

"There were some girls at high school that used to do it as well. It's not crazy," Ayumi replied dryly.

That morning at 5:45, the start of their two-hour journey to college, she and Ayumi had had a five-minute conversation about the fact that neither had completed their homework for class. Ayumi then fell asleep on her left arm, leaving her right hand free to reach and pull at her hair as the JR train softly rocked its way from Gifu to Nagoya. Her thoughts were of the recent conversation at work with her boss; the same employer that forbade her to dye her hair when she was hired.

"Please keep your black hair. Our business guests like to see hotel employees looking presentable," he said, having previously told her that she would be working in the kitchen away from the guests, not in the restaurant.

She had wanted to dye her hair blond when she first got to college, but when she saw the popular girls with their long blond tresses, she thought they would make fun of her for trying to look like them. And she would never look like them, she wasn't that pretty.

A medium brown color would have been acceptable. At the local *Daiso*, she had held up one of those fake brown hair attachments against her cheek. It only cost 100 yen for a lock and 300 yen for a brown ponytail. Looking into the store mirror, it had looked nice, she'd looked nice. However, her *arubaito* ended any change in color and she would have to stay with her plain black hair, a reminder of her school days.

Chizuro needed this job. Her parents weren't wealthy, and her mother always reminded her that they were paying her college fees. Out of her small salary, Chizuro paid for her lunch at the college cafeteria, and often dinner, via the *combini* before she embarked on her two-hour journey back home. She also bought her makeup, toiletries, clothes, shoes, gifts for her family and friends on birthdays; there was never enough to buy everything she needed or wanted.

Graduation was in five months and she still hadn't found a full-time job. Along with her class, she had gone through the job application and interview training provided by the college, filled out lengthy application forms for several employers, and managed to attend one group interview at a department store, but was rejected for the next interview level. Her mother wasn't happy to hear that she didn't even get to the second round of interviews.

"Keiko's daughter Emiko already has a job offer at Matsuzakaya. The college gave you the training, so what did you do at the interview? Were you polite? Did you show you would be a good worker? You have to try harder,

Chizu. Everyone has helped you. We sent you to a good college and your teachers have tried their best, but you have to try hard as well."

Her mother would never understand. It wasn't that she didn't try hard, but no matter what she did, she knew inside that she would never be the career girl her mother thought she could be.

On a Saturday afternoon, while cutting endless amounts of *daikon* in the kitchen of a hotel near Gifu station, having finished mopping the floor and stacking the glasses inside the cupboards, her boss had called her aside, informing her she could continue working there full-time after she graduated. Her salary would remain the same, seven hundred yen an hour, and she would have longer shifts.

"You're a good worker and I know it's hard to find a job today, too many graduates for one job. If you work here full-time, your family won't worry that you'll be at home all day without a job. What do you think?"

She'd replied, "Thank you, thank you very much Iwata-san, thank you, you're very kind," bowing her head many times, as was expected.

"Okaasan, Iwata san told me I can work full-time at the hotel after I graduate." She hoped her mother would be a little happy at her news, even though it wasn't an office job, it was still permanent employment. She stood in the kitchen, speaking to her mother's back, while her mother washed the dishes.

"What will you do?" Her mother asked, turning around. Chizuro faced her mother's quizzical expression, eyebrows furrowed. If she spoke the truth, her mother would get upset, but what else could she say?

"Ah, in the beginning, I'll do the same job as I do now, but maybe I'll get promotion after a few years and do other things. I'd like to work at the front desk. I could ask Iwata-san..."

Her mother's eyes looked away before turning around to complete her dishwashing task. There was silence.

That night in the quiet of her room, Chizuro dug her nails into the middle of her lower right arm until blood appeared. This was better than pulling her hair. Seeing blood, dark red blood, was reserved for special events. She should be happy that she had a full-time job before she had finished college; scratching a line from the freshly created sore down to her wrist. She should be happy that she didn't have to go through many company interviews with thousands of other girls her age; scratching the line over and over again until the red skin split and more blood appeared. She should be happy that she would earn more money and didn't have to learn any new skills at work; red blood began to trickle down her stinging arm. She should be happy that she had a mother even though her mother would never be happy with anything she did; reaching out for the tissues next to her bed and dabbing at the blood.

She was happy; the long line on her arm stopped bleeding.

Junko

Glancing at the discussion questions on the chapter titled, "Your Family", Junko became immediately irritated.

"This is a stupid textbook," she whispered in a low voice to Sayako as they sat in the hot, humid classroom. Wiping her face with a small wash rag covered with a *Totoro* print, she was careful not to smudge her thick black mascara and eyeliner, which she had painstakingly drawn around her eyes. It took her thirty minutes to do her makeup this morning in the rock style, reminiscent of American eighties girl bands. Then a further twenty minutes to gel her hair into neat spikes. She loved her new pixie-style hair with its long layers; it was natural black with one side section dyed bright red to resemble a lightning streak. She wanted to look like a tough girl, not a cute one.

Her severely ripped tight blue jeans seemed glued to her thin legs, and every time she moved them under the desk, the different sized metal rings and hooks that hung off her front belt loops made a dull thudding noise as they struck each other. She had known it was too hot to wear jeans that day, but they matched her black t-shirt with the loose neck, accentuating what she called her 'danger *rokku* look'. The white and red writing on her t-shirt proclaimed,

"I'm caught in rock dream and the spiritual is very hot."

When she had read those words on the four thousand yen t-shirt, it expressed exactly how she felt inside. She wanted to live the rock dream, to be bad, to have people look at her a little scared, and to be everything other than how she was raised.

"Atsui ne," she heard Chiyoe's voice behind her.

Most of her classmates had animation-printed washcloths like hers and were furiously wiping their moist faces, necks, and arms. The teacher was the only one who had a fan, probably from the 100-yen shop. Foreign teachers were always talking about how great those stores were in Japan.

The women's college only turned on the air conditioner when parents called in to complain that their daughters were feeling faint with the oppressive heat. It was already mid-June, the temperature was twenty-eight degrees centigrade with ninety percent humidity. *Why didn't anyone complain?* Probably because they had been given the same responses that her mother gave to her when she moaned about the sauna-like classrooms.

"Everyone has to save electricity since the earthquake. You mustn't be selfish, Junko, think of the people in Tohoku. Everyone in Japan must do their part. And why do you have to dress like that? It's not cute. People will be afraid when they see you." Her mother was always irritated by her clothes.

"But why does the main university have air conditioning and not our college? It's not fair," she continued, ignoring her mother's derisory comment on her sense of fashion.

"Because it's a more important place. The students are studying there for four years, it's not a junior college. Also, that's where the offices are found for the President and the administrators who work there, you should understand that. I'm sure they also turn their air conditioner down. Everyone is following the government's 'Cool Japan' program. Junko, you're going to be twenty soon, and when you become a woman you should know how to sacrifice, don't be selfish, think of others."

Think of others? She was tired of hearing that from her mother. She wanted to retort, "Did my father ever think of you?" But she knew better than to voice those thoughts aloud.

The words 'woman' and 'sacrifice' always went together for all the females in her mother's family. It must be a generation thing because neither she nor any of her friends thought like that. For her, the words 'woman' went together with 'fashion, money, and boyfriend'.

The soft-spoken American teacher who slowly enunciated every word caught her attention for less than a minute.

"Please turn to the person next to you. I only want to hear you speaking English. Please start."

Why did they have to learn English? They had already suffered years of English in high school. She thought the torture would end in college, but yet here she was, sitting in another stupid English class, and it wasn't even her major.

"Shit! How much longer do we have?" she groaned, turning to Sayako and resuming her usual level of speaking.

"Shh, thirty-five minutes more, then we can go outside," Sayako whispered back, smiling.

Good. It was time for a cigarette, some more chocolate, and a can of lemon tea. That was their own special diet which they had come up with themselves and had religiously stuck to for a year and a half. Two chocolate bars a day, one in the morning, one in the afternoon, two bars of *Calorie Mate* for lunch, two or three cans of cold lemon tea or green tea throughout the day, together with smoking half a pack of cigarettes.

In the evening, she would eat the meal her mother made for her. On weekends, the diet was relaxed. On Saturday, she bought a McDonald's fish meal set with ice cream for lunch, and then have soup for dinner. On Sunday, her grandmother usually brought a meal for both her mother and her. In high school, she was 45 kilos, which was too fat. On this diet, she was now a perfect 39 kilograms (86 pounds).

"Junko, English please, ask Sayako the questions," the teacher said.

"Okay, let's speak English!" she mocked the teacher in a raised voice, trying to impersonate one of the American voices she had heard on an English language DVD. The teacher always looked a bit afraid when she spoke aggressively like that and it made her want to do it more. "Sayako, what is your mother's name?" She continued speaking loudly, reading the question from the chapter.

Sayako giggled, as did most of the class. The teacher's face was serious.

"Be careful, Junko chan," Sayako warned her quietly in Japanese before saying aloud in English, "My mother's name is Hitomi."

"She can't do anything to me, apart from say 'English please'. Even if she gives me a bad grade, Nakamura san in the office will make her pass me," she responded in Japanese.

Behind her, she heard Chiyoe laugh at her comment, so she turned around to face her.

"It's true, right, Chiyo chan? They don't fail anyone in this college. It'll look bad for them."

Chiyoe nodded.

"Junko, come on, let's do this exercise, sensei is looking." Sayako pulled on her arm until she turned back around to face forward.

"Okay, Saya chan, ask me the next question," she said in Japanese.

"Junko, what does your father do?" Sayako asked, looking towards the teacher as if to prove that they could take the lesson seriously.

The question prompted Junko to switch back into Japanese, knowing that now was the time to tell her friend what had been happening in her home.

"I have to tell you something," she said quietly, noticing the teacher had turned her back to them, perhaps giving up on the idea that they would do the exercise. "It's a secret, but my parents got a divorce two months ago."

Sayako responded in the way she expected; an eye-widening, shocked face, and sympathetic voice complete with hand-touching.

"Oh, Junko chan, I'm so sorry. Really? They got divorced? That's difficult. Are you okay?"

Now the questions would start, and she couldn't avoid them. She knew a few other friends also had divorced parents, but no one talked about it openly. Sometimes in class, a student might say that she and her mother lived alone, and that was enough to stop more questions; the situation was understood. Another cue was if a girl said she didn't see her father much because he worked abroad. Sometimes it was true, but most times, it was an excuse to avoid having classmates tease you that you didn't have two parents at home and were somehow abnormal. Her mother had told her to say something similar if asked about her father.

"Junko, tell them he has to work in Osaka or Tokyo so no one will be suspicious." *As opposed to the truth that my father drank heavily after work with his boss, returned home on the last train, only to be immediately angered by something trivial, which would turn into shouting and throwing things, including my mother, around the house.*

"My mother doesn't talk about it much. I don't know everything that happened between them."

She knew enough but would never tell anyone *that* truth. Sayako would be told the sanitized version. "My mother told me a few months ago,

'Your father and I are getting a divorce. We're not happy together.' Then one weekend, she said they had divorced."

"Parents are strange. But that's hard for you," Sayako sympathized, looking as if she were about to cry.

"I'm okay. My father lives about fifteen minutes away."

She had visited only once when her mother had sent her with a cooked meal for him. She didn't understand why her mother cooked for her father after how he'd behaved, but her mother told her to take the meal for him, so she did.

Her father's mansion smelt like stale smoke and old food, and it was dirty. When she described it to her mother, her mother said, "Next time you should be a good daughter and clean it for him". However, Junko had decided she would only do it if he gave her more money.

Turning to Sayako, she explained, "My dad visits us every week to give us money. He gives us separately, so I'm lucky I don't need a part-time job." For her, that was the most positive side of her parents' divorce.

"But what about your mother? Does she cry? Is she upset?" Sayako asked.

"I don't know. She seems okay."

Her mother never talked about anything concerning emotions, all she did was criticize.

"This morning she was complaining about my clothes. She's doesn't understand fashion and young people. She's old, she'll be forty-five this year."

"Yes, my mother is the same. She always asks me what I'm going to do when I leave college. I say I want a job so I can have money to have fun, but she said it's better for me to be married," Sayako grumbled.

"Shit, I don't want to get married, later, maybe never." Junko had already decided living with one man for life wasn't for her.

"No, don't say that. We have to get married sometime."

"Why? What for?" *So he can hit me with his shoe or throw the soup I made for him against the wall when he comes home drunk?* "My father gives me money and if I get a boyfriend, I will also make him buy me things, otherwise I won't have sex with him."

Sayako burst out laughing at her bold remark, "You're bad, Junko."

"No, I'm not bad. I'm smart. My father has to pay for me because I'm his only child and when I get a boyfriend, he also has to pay for me, so I won't need a full-time career, only a part-time one. I don't need to get married for money because I can have it without getting married. I'm going to enjoy myself all the time. You should try and get your father to give you money, you're the only girl."

"I don't know. My parents want my brother to be a lawyer, so they're paying a lot of money for him to live in Osaka near to his university. But if I get a rich boyfriend, then maybe I'll be like you and won't need a full-time job."

"And we can go to parties and shop together every day. We can go on holiday to Okinawa and life will be fun."

Junko believed her plan would work. She would make it work. Her life would be different, it would be exciting. She would never be like her mother. She would never marry a man like her father.

Akemi

"I don't think I knew I was a lesbian for many years. I just knew I was different. I think my mother knew as well. She said when I was little, I didn't like any of the things that my older sister liked, such as playing with dolls, wearing dresses, even brushing my hair. I liked boy things. Even when I didn't know that something was meant for boys, I would have already liked it. I liked wearing comfortable clothes, boys' clothes, I wanted short hair, and I wanted to play with boys.

"My mother would tell me I was making too much noise when I ran around the house shouting and throwing my toys about. I remember her telling me to be quiet. When I think about my childhood, the number one thing I remember was being told to be quiet. Later, it was not only being quiet, but being told to be polite, which meant talking softly, or *kawaii*. What was so wrong with using my voice? I wasn't rude when I spoke, but I wouldn't talk all high-voiced and cute, so I suppose that meant that I wasn't being polite. I didn't understand at that time how all this related to not being girly. I still don't completely understand it. I could see the difference though when my mother and sister talked to other people. They changed their voices and the way they said things. They changed everything. I wanted to be the same all the time, not changing who I was.

"In junior high, I understood that I wasn't like most of the girls there, but for another reason. I came from a single-parent family. My parents were divorced, and we didn't see our father much. He lived in Tokyo and worked for a company selling things like calendars and paper goods. He sent gifts on our birthdays and for New Years, although when I got to high school, he began to send money, which was better for me.

"I don't know why my parents divorced because I was only about three or four when it happened. My mother never talked about him or why they divorced. The only thing she would say to me and my sister was, "You have a letter or package from Tokyo." I remember once hearing her say to my grandmother when they were in the kitchen and they didn't know I could hear from the living room,

"Even though it's difficult, I'm glad I got a divorce, it is better for all of us, better that the girls didn't see that side of him."

"On the few occasions when we saw our father over the years, he had the same attitude as my mother. He never spoke about why they divorced or asked about my mother.

"At elementary school, a few girls found out that my parents were divorced and would tell me, "You have no father, you're strange," or things like that. Once in junior high school, a group of girls surrounded me at the bus stop and kept calling me, "divorce child, divorce child." They also said, "You're weird, strange, you are not normal." I never said anything back to them at that time, but later I decided if anyone said anything to me, I'd shout, "I don't care."

"For the most part, a lot of the girls left me alone, apart from the girls in the soccer club; they were much nicer to me. The boys never teased me. If I had contact with boys, like have a conversation with one or two of them, they were always nice to me. Boys never said harsh things to me.

"When I think of junior high school, and especially my senior high school years, I thought all girls were stupid and mean. I hated them. They were always laughing with their high voices, screaming at photos of boys, being afraid of everything they were asked to do that was different. "*Kowai*, I'm scared, I'm scared," they would squeal. It was interesting that when girls were screaming like cats at boy bands or something like that, no one ever told them to be quiet.

"I had a few friends on the soccer team. Ryoko was my only friend throughout my school life. She was a tall girl and she used to get teased by other girls because of her height. She played on a lot of different sports teams when we were at junior high school. We met in the soccer club at junior high, and we also played soccer at high school together. Later, I dropped out of playing soccer, and so did she because she had to study for her final exams. I dropped out for another reason, but also for studying for exams.

"In class, I would sit at the back in the classroom on the side. Most of the teachers never bothered with me. I don't know why. Maybe because they knew about my parents. I rarely got called on in class, especially in high school, I was kind of invisible. It was only at soccer practice that I would hear my name called by the coach. I wasn't a star player, but the coach was nice to me, and I enjoyed practice and meeting my friends there. Soccer club was the best part of my school career.

"At home, my mother was annoyed when I said I wanted to play soccer in junior high school. She said my body would get too big, like a man, and that I would get muscles. I still joined the team though, and she bought me whatever I needed to play even though she would always complain about it. My sister, Yui, used to tease me about playing on the team and said only girls who were like men played soccer, but she wasn't like those girls at school, she didn't say it to be cruel. It was just her opinion because she never played sports or anything like that.

" Yui was three years older than me and we were so different. I don't think my mother could understand why. No one did, not even me. When she was studying for her final exams in high school, my mother was always concerned about her. How much sleep she got, what food she ate, and they went to the temple a lot to pray for Yui's success in her exams.

"My mother wanted Yui to get a scholarship to go to this expensive women's college, so when she graduated, she would get a good office lady job at a big company and marry an executive there. That was my mother's plan and Yui more than agreed. My mother didn't talk about her plan for me.

"By the time I got to high school, Yui was in college. She didn't get into her first-choice college, but her second choice instead. At first, my mother was a bit upset, but then she found out that this college also had good job prospects for my sister, so her plan could still be carried out. However, the college fee was expensive, and my mother and Yui were worried about how to pay for it. I also worried because I knew how much it meant to my sister and mother that Yui goes to this college. Yui already had a part-time job at a *combini* to help with some expenses. So it wasn't as if she was expecting my mother to pay for everything.

"In the end, Yui contacted my father and asked him if he would pay for some of the fees, and he said he would pay for all of it, but only if my mother paid for my college fees. My mother agreed and said that it would be cheaper for her because there was no point in sending me to a prestigious women's college since I wasn't like my sister. I don't know exactly what she meant by that, but at the same time, I did. She was only being honest, as I would never be the kind of daughter who got excited about receiving all those cute blouses and pink nail polishes she bought for Yui.

"As for me, high school started like my junior high school life had. I joined the soccer club with Ryoko, and I spent the rest of my time studying or watching TV. I didn't like studying that much, and I didn't fail many exams, maybe one or two. I didn't get high grades, but I didn't care, and no one else did either.

"I didn't have many friends because I didn't like most of the girls in my class, so I didn't care if I was friends with them or not. I knew they talked about me and laughed at me sometimes. I could hear them saying, "She's ugly, she looks like a man." I didn't look like a man. I wasn't tall or had big muscles, but I didn't wear make-up or spend hours fixing my hair. One girl asked me if I looked the way I did because my parents were divorced. I said yes because it seemed easier to say yes than no and then get asked more questions.

"Why did I drop out of the soccer club? First, it was a big commitment and it was getting more difficult to ask for extra money from my mother for expenses to play at games in other towns.

"Soccer is not for girls your age. Look at you, you're getting muscles. You will look like a boy, and then what kind of future will you have?"

"Sometimes she would say, "I don't have money for those things. It's hard for me to support you and your sister. Your sister needs to have a car to go to college. All the other girls drive there and it's important for her not to feel different from other girls as it can affect her future. Do you have to play on the team?"

"The second reason I dropped from soccer was my size. In high school, my daily life changed. I used to go straight home after soccer practice, or if I didn't have practice, I'd go straight home after class. My mother would usually be home by then.

"But at the end of 10th grade, my mother got a promotion and became a supervisor. She had to work longer hours and wasn't home when I got back. She began to give me money to get something to eat for the evening. I took the subway home as my high school was not on a bus line, and at the subway station there were many places to eat, such as Subway, McDonald's, Mister Donuts, 7-11, and Circle K.

"My family used to eat McDonald's every now and then, especially if we went out on the weekend, and I liked it. When my mother gave me money, I would always go to McDonald's because they gave the most food for the smallest amount of money, and it tasted delicious.

"By the 11th grade, I told my mother I could get my dinner most times, and she was happy about that. Honestly, it became the best part of my day. I'd look forward to trying different McDonald's meals. The taste was so good that sometimes I wished I could eat it for every meal, although I knew it wasn't very healthy.

"My weight, my size, had gone up at the end of 10th grade, and my coach said I had to be careful about it. In the second month of 11th grade, I told my coach I couldn't be on the team anymore because I had to study for exams. My mother was very happy to hear this. I was also happy because it meant that after school I could go to McDonald's and relax. It was the best time of the day for me. Ryoko didn't always come with me, so I was by myself. It was okay. I liked to sit, eat, and play games on my phone. Sometimes I couldn't wait to get out of class so I could go to McDonald's I'd stay there for 2 or 3 hours until my mother called and said she was home.

"By the time I got to 12th grade, my size was about double of what I was in 10th grade; my weight was high for Japanese, maybe not for Americans. Students called me fat. I didn't care. I still don't care what people think of me. My mother kept saying, "You're fat, you can't get a job, you can't get married," and my sister began to say the same. They didn't understand I didn't care to get a job in a department store welcoming customers, all day bowing and bowing, and having to look perfect with perfect make-up like those models in the *Shiseido* adverts with their perfect hair in a bun. I didn't want to work for Toyota making tea for the managers and talking in that stupid voice. I hated all of that.

"I refused to speak in a high voice. Why did I have to change my voice? I remember some girls in school had normal voices, but when they got a job or went to college, their voices got higher, like my sister's. When we were younger, everyone said my sister and I sounded the same, but now her voice is so high and cute. I didn't like those cute voices. They sounded like cartoons.

"It was funny, but the first time that I understood I was lesbian was when I was sitting in McDonald's reading about how to lose weight. I knew I was getting bigger and I didn't want to be *metabo*, overweight, so I was reading these posts about why women got fat. There was one post from this woman. She said that Japanese women were obsessed with weight and being thin; it was not mentally healthy. She said girls were becoming anorexic because of the pressure to be thin and that society had to change this thinking. She also wrote that this thinking came from men's opinions of women. I had never really read anything like that before, but I understood it, I agreed with it.

"Underneath her comment, another person wrote she was stupid to have this opinion and she was a feminist because she hated men; the next comment said something similar. Below that was a comment from a woman who said feminists don't hate men and that she agreed with what the first woman had said. I kept reading the comments, they were as interesting as the original post. Then the original poster wrote and said that she was a feminist, that she didn't hate men, although she was a lesbian. She wrote about something called negative self-image and talked about how many women believed these images. More than that, they often attacked other women who didn't conform to those ideas. It was like students at school attacking me for how I looked.

"I wished I could have met that woman, she sounded so cool. If that's what a lesbian or a feminist thought, then I liked them, and maybe I was one, too. I began to search online and read and read about feminism and lesbianism. I read many stories about girls who sounded like me growing up. In fact, there were many girls like me.

"When I was at college, I was bigger than I was in 12th grade, but I didn't care. I tried not to eat McDonald's all the time, but it was hard. The teachers at my college were nice, I was so surprised. Many of them knew my name and asked me questions in class. I especially liked my English teachers. One of them was from America, and she treated all of us very kindly. More girls were nice there as well, not like in high school, girls that I didn't expect to like with their high voices and constant laughing. I even made a best friend there. Her name was Mayuri, and she told me her parents were also divorced. We talked about all kinds of things. I told her, after we became good friends, that I didn't like girls like her in high school. She was very slim and pretty, *kawaii,* but she was very kind to me and always helped me in class. We had lunch together every day.

"I also got a part-time job at Circle K because Mayuri introduced me to her high school friend who knew the manager. I still work there. During college, I worked nights and weekends, and I began saving my money because I wanted to live in my own apartment. My mother was happy that I got a part-time job and that I liked my college. But she still thought I was fat and complained that she could never find clothes for my size.

"When I told her that I had been trying to save money to live on my own because I wanted to be independent, I was shocked when she said, "I will be lonely if you leave." My sister works in Osaka, so she doesn't live at home anymore.

"I could never tell my mother or sister that I'm a lesbian. I have a few lesbian friends that I met online on this members-only website, and we meet once a month at a bar. We text and email about all kinds of things, even about the girls we like. I love being with these friends because I am completely myself.

"Maybe in the future, I will tell Mayuri that I'm a lesbian, she might know already, and I don't think she will judge me. We talked about gay people before and she said society should not discriminate against gay people.

"I don't know what my future is, but I'm happy that I know who I am. Perhaps life will be difficult for me because my friends say you can never tell people that you're lesbian, but that's okay. If life is like this for lesbians, it's still better than being called strange because your parents are divorced or because you're fat."

Aiko

"My name means love child or love girl. I am love!" Aiko said in her perfected American accent, beaming her model smile at the only foreign male teacher at their college. He had asked them to find out why their parents had given them their names and their meanings. She hadn't bothered to ask her parents, everyone knew what her name meant.

The fact was, education, let alone English classes, were not her first priority now, not even her second. She only showed up to classes out of some sense of duty towards her parents because they were paying to see her graduate, and because she didn't want to see 'Fail' written on any of her courses. It was a matter of pride for both her and her parents.

Now in the final semester of her two-year English communications degree, Aiko had begun to feel a sense of freedom as she had before she graduated from high school.

In those last months of high school, unlike many of her friends, she didn't have to take the grueling university entrance exams, only a simple entrance test for the women's college; one which she passed with ease and without studying. Then she began her summer of metamorphosis, in which the first stage was to dye her hair golden brown with the money her grandmother gave her as a high school graduation present.

"Ai chan, you look beautiful," said her younger sister as she entered through the front door with her newly-colored hair.

"Eeeh, like a model!" exclaimed her mother.

From the compliments of the two females in the house, and to the eventual praises from other people around her, Aiko changed her outer self.

By the time she entered college in September, she was unrecognizable from the high school student of four months ago. Mastering the walk of a catwalk model through YouTube videos, her body looked more poised and elegant. She changed her eye color to a light hazel via contact lenses paid for by her mother. Her clothes were carefully chosen to parallel a European sophisticated look, not the cute look that most Japanese girls favored.

In her first English class at college, she comfortably rattled off a detailed self-introduction without once looking at the textbook example.

"I studied English very hard because I wanted to be an interpreter and work for the government or the Japanese embassy. That is still my goal and why I came to college. I want to work with both Japanese and foreign people. My parents also helped me because they paid for extra English classes with a foreign teacher. She was from Michigan and was friendly, but strict. She told me to watch American movies without subtitles and listen to English songs to try and understand the words. I wrote out the lyrics of many songs after listening to them twenty or thirty times. My sister asked me why I didn't look for them on Google, but I wanted to understand the sentences, to see if they used the present or past tense, and to learn new words."

This fluent explanation, combined with her half-manufactured, half-natural attractiveness, ensured that she exuded a confidence lacking among her classmates. She thought most of them looked like misplaced high school students with their impulsively-bought clothes and silly giggles. Furthermore, they could not speak one sentence in English without having to be told what to say. It was obvious why teachers paid her more attention. She overheard them call her mature and intelligent when speaking to their colleagues in the college corridors.

"You're very pretty, are you a model?" asked a suited man in a quiet voice.

That was how Aiko got her part-time job at the club. She had been sashaying along the street with Yuka and Noriko on a Saturday evening. They had shopped and Starbuck'ed during the day, as was their usual weekend habit. Then before going to the dance club, they stopped for *takoyaki* and beer to get them into a happy mood. Having celebrated *Seijin No Hi* a few months ago, they were all of age to freely drink, smoke, and drive.

Aiko didn't drive and didn't smoke as she believed it was bad for her skin, but she drank. She'd had her first beer the second week of the first semester of college when she'd visited her two new friends, Yuka and Noriko, who lived in the student residences. They were not under parental supervision as she was.

"Drink more. It's fun to get drunk," urged Noriko after Aiko had her first sip of beer.

"It doesn't taste good," she muttered.

"Drink a lot at one time and then eat some *yakitori*, it makes the flavor good."

Soon Aiko was giggling, and her head felt strange. By the end of the first semester, she had been drunk regularly, often before they went out to the clubs, and had thrown up a couple of times in Noriko's house.

The suited man, Manabe san, was part-owner of a small club in the city.

"Do you have a job?" he asked, looking at Aiko intensely and ignoring her two friends.

"Why?" she asked boldly. "I'm a student. I'm studying English. I don't need a job." Which wasn't completely truthful as her mother had recently commented,

"Aiko chan, it would be good to have an *arubeito,* because part-time work can help you become a *shakai-jin*, a person of society."

Aiko looked at this man and for a second in her tipsy state contemplated that she should tell him to get lost, but something about his serious demeanor stopped her and she listened.

"I can offer you part-time work if you want to work at my club. I'll pay you a salary and you'll get tips from clients. It's a high-quality club and you have the right look. If you're interested, call me. What's your name?" He didn't smile as he spoke to her.

"Aiko. Tsuda, Aiko," as she took his *meishi*. His business card read, "Manabe, Hiroyuki" printed in large kanji, and below the club name, "Star Venus".

A few days later, without telling anyone, Aiko called Manabe san to set up an interview, and within a week, had started her new job as a hostess for *Staru Benusu*.

Yuka and Noriko knew she worked at the club. She told her parents that she would be staying with them at the weekend. She originally worked on Friday and Saturday nights from eight o'clock to about four or five in the morning. After two months, she began working two nights during the week as well.

Her college work was nowhere near demanding, due to her English level being far advanced for the classes. She barely did homework or any form of study. She simply showed up to class, most times with a hangover from the night before, but nevertheless, still receiving admiration from her friends and teachers for being able to complete the classwork quickly and correctly.

College was not as she had originally thought it would be. Some English classes were interesting, but overall, she wasn't challenged and learned very little. Her career advisor, Otake san, suggested she think about working in a company office or trying for a job in a travel agency.

"It's difficult to get jobs in an embassy or an international company because you don't have any other skills. You're good at English, but you need to have a four-year degree, so you must transfer to the main university and graduate from there. Even so, it's very difficult for a student, a woman, to get this kind of job. I strongly suggest that you try to work for a small travel company. You dress very nicely, and you can easily demonstrate that you can speak English to their international customers."

"Thank you, Otake san." She knew there was no need to take the advice; she had no intention of working at a travel agency.

"What do you have to do in the club?" asked an inquisitive Yuka one evening while they shaved each other's eyebrows with small pink eyebrow shavers. "Are all the men old? Do you have to do anything with them?"

"No, it's not *soupurando*!" Aiko retorted disparagingly.

"I know, but you hear stories," replied Yuka.

"Most of the men are old, but it's not so bad. I had a few men touch my leg under the table, and that was all. The first time I didn't know what to do, and I told Kameko, my *sempai.* She said that's all they will do, touch your leg under the table. But every time it happened, I got a really big tip."

"Eeeh! how much extra did you get?"

"Five thousand yen, sometimes *ichi man yen*. The work is easy, all I do is drink, talk, laugh, and sometimes sing. When we get there, all of us hostesses stand near the bar. The customer can ask for a specific hostess, or if he doesn't, then we all take turns talking with him for about fifteen minutes each, making sure his glass is full. That's the most important thing; his glass must always be filled.

"I have three regular customers who ask for me. Two of them love to sing karaoke with me. It's funny because I taught them how to pronounce the English words in some of the songs, and so they always request me. My other client is a company director, and when he found out that I was majoring in English, he brought this manager from the Philippines to talk with me. I made so much money that night. They both come every two or three weeks and it's my best night for money.

"Also, I don't have to buy any drinks. The customers pay for mine as well as theirs. My first few nights I got so drunk because when a client buys you a drink, you have to accept and drink it. After she saw me getting sick, Kameko told me that I should order grape juice, not wine, that's what a lot of girls do. You tell the bartender, and they know what to pour for you, but the clients think they are paying for wine, not grape juice. I can drink a lot more than when I first started, remember how I used to be?" she said, laughing. "Shall I tell you a secret? I have so much money in my account now. I have enough to visit America or Australia. I'm sure if I work at Club Venus full-time, I'll be able to earn more than an office lady, more like an OL manager. When we graduate, I am going to ask Manabe san if I can work full-time. He said I'm a good worker, but I have to keep my looks nice. Kameko told me she works six nights a week, and there's a mansion available in her building that I can live in if I want to move; it's near to the club."

"But I thought you wanted to transfer to the main university. And what about your parents?" Yuka asked.

"There's no point being a student for two more years and not have a job after. Now I can work at the club. I don't need to tell my parents what my job is. I tell them I work in a kind of restaurant-bar."

"But what about your future and working for an embassy?"

"Future? I can't get a job at an embassy, it's too difficult. Anyway, when I talk English with some of the foreign customers, it's almost like working in an embassy. I practice my English and I learn new words from them. I'm glad I'm doing this job. If I got a job in a company or a department store, it would be a difficult life for me. In this job, I don't need to study or think about anything. I get a salary plus tips. I dress in nice clothes, get free drinks all night, sometimes food, and I have fun. This is my future."

Haruko

"I can't go in," she cried.

"Are you sure? Okay, maybe tomorrow we will try again," her mother said gently.

Haruko knew her mother was drained with her behavior, but this time she really thought she could do it. It was now the fifth week of school and she had yet to attend a full week of college, plagued as she was by these attacks.

Looking back, she couldn't quite remember when she first experienced the fear of entering college. She used to dread her final year of high school, standing at the gates, stomach aching, lips dry, yet she always managed to walk in. Then, after a few routine trips to the bathroom to calm down, she would finally take her seat near the back row and get through the rest of the day without any further problems.

On the first day of the summer after high school graduation, she decided to take her parents' advice and relax. They told her she deserved a break for studying so hard these last few years, and she agreed by staying in her room that day.

It was wonderful not to do anything or to think anything. No more waking up at 5:00 a.m. to go to school; no more listening to teachers drone on about unconnected details in world history that wouldn't stay in her mind long enough to pass the tests; no more mother trying out different meals that supposedly help the teenage brain to retain more information; no long nights of studying until midnight; and no more prayers at the temple for exam success. She had been accepted to a prestigious women's college, which had programs where she could study abroad if she wanted; a college that boasted a ninety percent job find rate for their graduates. By entering this college, she had shown everyone that she was able to be successful. Her future was set.

Lying on the bed on her first free day, she spent hours deciding how she should change her room, her clothes, and her hair. Her mother called her downstairs twice that day for lunch and dinner, and as soon as she was finished, she returned to the comfort of her room.

"*Onesan*," calling to her elder sister a few days later, "if you're going to the store, could you buy me some hair dye please?"

"You need to go to the hair salon if you want to change your color because they need to lighten it, after that you can use a box dye. You want me to make an appointment for you?" her sister asked her from the downstairs kitchen.

"No, it's okay. I can call later." She wanted to look online at the summer hair fashions to be able to tell the stylist exactly what she wanted.

A week went by and she stayed at home, watching daytime soap operas, and texting or talking on Skype to her friends, Mao and Natsumi.

"Haruko chan, you look different since graduation," Natsumi said via Skype.

"How do you mean?" she asked, not knowing whether this was a good or bad thing.

"You look happy. It's nice; before you looked tired. Maybe we all did," her friend added.

"I am happy. This is the best vacation I have ever had. I wake up when I want, go to sleep when I like, eat, drink, and watch television in my pajamas all day if I want. It's perfect." She smiled.

"Oh, I can't do that every day, I get bored. I want to go out. Let's go shopping this week."

Natsumi always wanted to do something, and when the time came to go out, Haruko decided against it. It looked like it would rain, and she really wanted to watch her now favorite afternoon soap opera.

Five weeks later, no one paid attention to the fact that she hadn't left the house. Her father worked all day and came home late at night. Her older sister worked in a pharmacy and came home to eat dinner, then went out again with her friends. Her mother worked part-time and was gone in the mornings. Even Haruko herself hadn't realized that she had been indoors all this time.

It wasn't like she hadn't tried to go outdoors. She did. Twice. But each time, her stomach started acting up, reminding her of what it had been like waiting outside the school gates. She knew she was never going to go to school again, but something about putting on her shoes in the *genkan* made her heart thud against her blouse and her whole body felt shaky. At that point, she decided she didn't need to go out, and turned around and went back to her room.

"Haruko chan, shall I make an appointment for you at the hair salon, I'm going today. You can change your color in time for college," her mother asked her from downstairs. Her mother faithfully went to the salon every six weeks.

"It's okay. I'll go later," she replied. College was starting in two weeks.

"But we need to get you some new clothes for the new semester, let's go on Monday," her mother insisted.

That Monday, Haruko wore her peach pleated cotton skirt with a white blouse that had a sailor-type collar. Her shoulder-length hair was still black with a few long grays in it; a leftover sign from examination hell. She also needed new glasses, as everything looked a bit blurry.

As she walked into the *genkan* and bent down to put on her shoes, her mouth became dry and her stomach got tight. Fighting the feeling of wanting to run back upstairs to her bedroom, she put her hand on the door handle. A great fear rose up in her chest and paralyzed her, she stood there in front of the door not knowing what to do.

What seemed like thirty minutes was probably only five, but she was awakened out of her panic daze by the door opening, and her mother, who had got fed up with waiting in the car, appearing at the front door.

"What's the matter? Come on, the traffic will be bad." Perhaps something in her face told her mother that all was not well. "Haruko, what's wrong? Let's go," and her mother took her hand.

"Nooooo." The voice came from somewhere within her chest. "I can't, nooooo." And without removing her shoes, she pulled away from her mother's hand and ran back upstairs to her room, her lovely comfortable room.

"I'm so sorry, Haruko isn't well again," she heard her mother explaining to the office ladies who had come to the main college entrance door to help. Haruko sat outside the college on the bench; a few girls walked by and tried not to look in her direction, but she knew they were talking about her.

"We took her to the doctor, and he said she has a kind of agoraphobia. It's all in the letter that the doctor gave us to give to you at the college. We hope she'll get better soon, but it seems she has some fear of college. Thank you for being so understanding, you're very kind. Please thank the director, Tanaka san, for his assistance," her mother continued.

When she arrived back home, her mother went to make some tea so she could take it with her medication. She turned on her computer and saw that Sayuri, her high school and now college *sempai*, had sent an email.

"I saw you today from the window of English Listening class. I hope you'll feel better soon and will be able to enjoy college life."

She looked for the first email she had received from Sayuri, when she had been at high school.

Haruko chan, college work isn't so difficult, it's fun. I recommend you take the English classes with the foreign teachers because they're much more interesting than the Japanese teachers' classes. The teachers always want you to speak in English, so it's a little bit difficult, but even if you don't understand, they'll help you pass their classes.

We also have an ikebana class, and there is a personal development class where they tell you about office life and how to make different kinds of coffee and tea. I liked that class because we were allowed to taste so many kinds of coffees and teas. The teachers at the college are very kind and friendly, you'll like it. It's not like high school.

I'm looking forward to seeing you in September.

She remembered the first time she had read that email, how excited she'd been. Sayuri hadn't written regularly, but whenever she did, she always spoke of the fun she was having at college and how the classwork wasn't stressful, quite the opposite.

But maybe Sayuri found the work easy. How could she be sure that she would? Suppose it was like high school, all the studying and exams to pass? And even when she started college, she would have to start looking for a job and go through all the interviews with thousands of other graduates. Then, if she got a job, she would have to train at her company, go through tests, it would be like another form of high school, another form of college. It was too much, too stressful. She wanted to throw up thinking about it. It was better to stay at home and be comfortable. She could always learn about *ikebana*, and coffees and teas, on the internet. She could learn English as well. Perhaps she could convince her mother that she could stay home and learn everything online. She really didn't need or want to go out at all.

Reiko

"I don't like to see a woman dressing like a man, talking with a deep voice, or using impolite words. We are women, we should be like women. Maybe it's okay for some because they are younger and it's different for them. But I really don't like to see women like this. I don't like to hear *rezubian*. It's not a good word."

At the age of 26, married for four years and her son Eiji approaching his third birthday, Reiko pondered for a short moment over her cup of black coffee, her shoulder-length, neatly-styled hair temporarily falling in front of her oval youthful face.

"But the truth is..." her voice trailed off as she raised her head to gaze through the large French-styled window of Café Du Rien, momentarily indulging in the seclusion of the leafy side street, a 30-second walk from crowded *Kawaramachi dori* heaving with its mandatory Saturday afternoon shoppers.

She continued looking out at the street aware that Yoshie, the 27-year-old well-traveled manager of a trendy Kyoto fashion store, was patiently sitting opposite, waiting for her to disclose 'the truth' as if they both didn't already know.

"I always liked, loved women, from when I was young. I don't love men in this way, not even my husband."

It was only recently that she had begun to voice her truth. It began when she became involved with a charity group that helped women who were experiencing hardships due to divorce or other domestic problems. The group was run by Saki, editor of a local bi-cultural women's magazine, who also happened to be the unofficial coordinator of women-only parties held monthly at a small bar.

Reiko had gone to the first party, a lively event filled with stimulating women and inspiring wine, and was stunned when she encountered two women kissing and embracing in the hallway outside of the bathroom. The couple, oblivious to her stares, could barely imagine what was rushing through her mind at that time as the initial shock transformed into another emotion.

Later, while lying on the futon next to her son Eiji, she wondered if that could ever be her. Concluding it was highly unlikely that she could ever be that expressive with another woman in public, nevertheless the sense of mental freedom that she felt, lulled her to sleep for that night and many more. Until the second party, and then the third, where she met Yoshie.

She was sipping a glass of wine and nodding her head in time with the music when she caught Yoshie smiling at her. A returned smile brought Yoshie over to her side, and an interesting conversation ensued about Yoshie's study abroad in Canada, followed by how she came to manage the small fashion store in one of the underground Kyoto malls. Yoshie came from a world that Reiko had barely experienced.

“Yoshie, you’re truly an independent career woman, I admire you,” she said to her after two large glasses of wine. She wanted to add, “You’re a brave woman, I wish I could be like you,” but she didn’t.

“Can I have another black coffee, please?” Yoshie asked the café waitress with a warm smile. “Reiko?”

“No, I’m okay, thank you.”

“So, does he know?” Yoshie asked quietly.

“Takayuki? I don’t know. I don’t think so. How would he know? He's at work all the time. Eiji is at my mother's twice a week, like now, and Taka knows I have my evenings to go out with my friends. As for anything else, well, I told him from the beginning I didn't like physical things, you know."

The infrequent sexual encounters she'd had with her husband stopped after she found out she was pregnant with Eiji.

"I don't get it. Why do you stay with him?" Yoshie looked at her as if she genuinely didn't understand, even though Reiko had explained it before.

"Because I'm his wife, we're married. We have a child together. This isn't Canada, or maybe you forgot that this is Japan." Reiko couldn't hide the admonishing tone in her voice. However, she immediately regretted it as she saw Yoshie's expression change from a wide-eyed questioning look to one of resignation. Perhaps she had gone too far.

"I haven't forgotten where I come from; being a foreign student was the biggest reminder of who I was," replied Yoshie. "So you would still stay married even though you're les... not straight?"

"Straight, gay, I never understood why there are these words. I don't think I am this word or that word. I am Japanese, a woman, a mother, a wife, these are more important words in life."

"But you also love women, Reiko," Yoshie whispered. "You might not like the words or definitions, you might not want to accept them, but it's part of who you are. I know what it's like. I know. My family, my mother, my friends, constantly asking me if I have a boyfriend, when am I going to get married? It's not easy to fight against it."

"But you're a career woman. People will understand."

"Understand what? You think it's easier for me?"

"Yes, it is." Reiko knew without a doubt that it was. "People know that career women are more, well, they have a more open mind, and you studied abroad, so you are an international person. I'm more ordinary, a housewife, a traditional woman. I went to junior college and learned flower arranging and tea ceremony. I met Takayuki at the neighboring university, and both of our families knew that it was only a matter of time before we got married. Reiko, I don't regret getting married and having Eiji, and it doesn't matter who I like or don't like. I wanted to have my life this way. It's the right thing for everyone, for us, for our families, even for society. How would life go on if we didn't get married and have children?"

Yoshie shook her head a few times before asking, "So what about us? You know I like you and you like me, that's why we're here now. Is this how things will be for the future?"

"Yes. It's best for everyone. What can I do? I can't do anything. This is my life and it's best to keep things this way. If you can't accept it, well then, I don't know. This is my life."

"You will never divorce Takayuki? Many women are divorced today; there's no shame in that."

"No, no divorce. If I divorce, I'll have to work, and women can't get jobs in this economy, especially women with young children. Then I'll have to get a place to live, and everything will be harder for me and Eiji. This is the best way."

"This is why Saki said it was hard to be with a Japanese woman unless they are Japanese, but not really Japanese. Remember her saying that?"

Reiko nodded. At one of the parties, Saki had been talking about how lesbians needed to raise their public profile because it would help individual women feel more confident about rejecting the life that society had set out for them. "She said we will only be half happy in Japan, never full happy, because too many lesbians are afraid to come out or they simply accept half happiness."

"I'm not afraid, Yoshie, and this is about doing the right thing for everyone. Do you want me to destroy Taka's life, Eiji's life, my parents' and friends' lives? Even my life? And why? A person can never be fully happy if it comes from making so many others unhappy. We must accept our situations. You and I must be happy with our half happiness.

Asami

I didn't want to go to a four-year university because I didn't like to study. I didn't want to be a career girl and work for a company, so there was no need for me to study for so long. I didn't know what I wanted to do after high school, maybe something in fashion because I loved dressing up, doing my nails, and going shopping. I like nice things, eating nice food at good restaurants. My friends always teased me and said I was like royalty because of how I dressed and spoke. I think it's important to always look and act sophisticated.

I like high fashion and spend my money on good things. I read that it is better to buy one expensive, classic item of clothing rather than lots of cheap clothes. It's the same with jewelry. I know that some people think I come from a rich family because of how I behave. I never tell them the truth. They can think those things. It's good for me that they think I'm different and wealthy. It means that I can give a good image to the world.

Since leaving high school and coming to college, I spend a lot of time reading about things that I think will be important for my future. My mother always told me that I should learn everything I could at college that will help me become successful in life, and that's why I took every class in tea ceremony, ikebana, English, and child psychology for when I have children. I try very hard to study English because I need to know the world's most important language, as well as the different courtesies and table manners from England.

Many girls my age don't think those things are necessary, but I do. I want to know the different ways to greet guests in English. I always tell my friends, it's more than, "Hello, pleased to meet you." Sometimes you need to be able to say, "Thank you for inviting us to dinner," or "It was a real pleasure spending time with you." I ask them what would happen if your future husband takes you to dinner with other international businesspeople? You need to know what to say, what cutlery to use, what clothes to wear, all of those things are very important to both of you.

Sometimes wives can make problems for their husbands if they don't know how to behave. I saw an American television program where the wife was from a country area. Her husband was wealthy and from the city, and she embarrassed him in front of his family and friends because she didn't know their ways. It was a comedy and even though everyone was laughing, in reality, that would be a terrible situation. I would never want to be like that wife.

Every morning, I spend at least two hours getting ready to come to college. I like things to match and look in order, but not like career girls with their boring white shirts and black suits. There's no fashion in that. They all look like robots.

Students don't know how to dress. They don't think about how the clothes relate to each other. Even if I wear jeans and a t-shirt, it still looks better than most of the girls at college because I know what accessories to wear with them. I match my makeup and hairstyle to my clothes, so the look is total and complete. It's about creating an image, an environment that matches your mood.

I believe that it doesn't matter that you're coming to college, you should use this time to practice how you should be, how you want to be seen when you become a *shakai-jin*, a person of our society. It's what I always tell my boyfriend Naoto. Sometimes we argue because he doesn't understand my viewpoint. He says I'm always thinking about how I look to other people, but it's not true, it's about how I want others to see me. I think there is a difference.

This is how I met Naoto. Many of my friends went to the same university after high school. But I came here because my high school friend Chie told me about it. She said it was on the same campus as the four-year university and there were many cute boys, so we could get boyfriends easily. This four-year university is very expensive. Everyone knows about it as it has an important name. Many wealthy students come here, so I thought it was a good place for me to attend because the students would have similar attitudes as me.

I told my parents in my last year at high school that I wanted to go to this college, and my mother took me to the open campus day. We were both impressed. My parents were happy with me attending here because they would only pay two years of college for me. My brother wanted to be a lawyer and my parents were able to pay more for him at university. It was a good decision for everyone.

When I arrived here, Chie and I didn't get a chance to meet the boys from the university, and when we did meet them, I didn't really like those that I saw. I thought they would be cuter and behave better, but they seemed childish. Then Chie said that her friend went to another university in Aichi and they were having a student festival. So we got tickets, and that's where I met Naoto.

From the moment I saw him, I thought he was very cool because he was tall, and he spoke very kindly. He was a friend of Chie's friend. He asked about our college and I told him he should visit us, but not on our campus, because boys are not allowed there. Instead, the next week, he visited the four-year university as he had a friend there. Chie and I walked up from our college to meet him in the cafeteria. I dressed very nicely on that day. After that, we texted and then he became my boyfriend.

Naoto's parents are doctors and they pay for his *mansion,* so he lives by himself, which is good for us. On Valentine's Day, he cooked a meal for me and gave me a gold bracelet. It's very expensive, but I wear it every day. That's when I knew we would get married.

I didn't tell my mother about Naoto for a while, and he said he wouldn't tell his family about me either. It was our secret. We'd meet two or three times a week after our classes and I would go to his apartment. At first, we only slept together; we didn't have sex for about two months. Then one evening, Naoto said we should try. It was strange because I thought it would be like in the movies. But I didn't make the screaming noises that women made in the movies. I stayed quiet as I didn't know what I should do exactly. Now it is much better because I've read many ways on the internet about how to make Naoto happy with sex.

I think the best thing we did together in his *mansion* when we first started dating, was to make meals for each other. Sometimes Naoto cooked and sometimes I did, sometimes we made our meal together. It was very romantic. I told my friends that Naoto cooked for me. They all thought I was so lucky. We never saw a man cook for a woman before. We also watched movies together and talked about future plans. It was, still is, a perfect relationship.

When it was my birthday, I finally told my mother I had a boyfriend. At first, she was surprised and asked where I met him. I told her about the student festival and that he was 21, a year older than me, and studied accountancy. She seemed happy that I had a boyfriend whose parents were doctors and were from Nagoya. That was important. My family is from Nagoya, and Nagoya families must keep together because they have different traditions from Tokyo people. Of course, they're not like Osaka people. I don't think Osaka families are as cultured or sophisticated as Nagoya families.

I also met Naoto's parents and brother, and they were very nice to me. His mother asked me when I was graduating and if I wanted to study more. I didn't really want to study anymore, but I told her I would like to study languages, especially French. She had been to Paris and said, "Bon jour, comment ca va?" I was surprised, but I remembered a French word, "merci," so I said that and she seemed happy I was able to understand. I also spoke a little English to his father, who has traveled all over the world. Naoto told me his parents were very impressed with me.

Their house is big. It has two floors and a staircase like an American house. The house had a mix of furniture from Canada and Japan. I liked this. It shows that his parents have an international mind. They are traditional, but modern as well. My family is a little too traditional, old-fashioned.

Naoto will graduate in a year, and I will graduate in four months. I thought I might look for a job at a department store or a designer fashion store. But we had a seminar at our college a few months ago, and the speaker told us it was very difficult to get jobs like that. There were hundreds, sometimes thousands of girls who wanted a job in Takashimaya, or to work at Yves Saint Laurent.

When Naoto graduates, his father has a friend who has already told him he can come to work at his company. At first, Naoto wanted to work at a big company, but he was also told how difficult it was to find a job at a large company in Nagoya, and that he would probably have to move to Tokyo or Osaka. I didn't want him to move and neither did he, so he decided to accept the job offer from his father's friend. I think it's a good idea, especially now that things have changed.

Chie and Yumi know, and Naoto's best friend knows. It's a secret, but I'm pregnant. I'm happy and so is Naoto, but we haven't told our families yet. Chie told me that the college won't let me graduate if they know I'm pregnant. If I was married, the college might give me permission.

I'm three months pregnant and our exams are in two months. I don't think anyone at college will know. I looked on the internet and know what kind of clothes to wear so my stomach does not look big. I'm also on a diet, so no one will be able to tell for months, maybe only in the last month.

When I had baby sickness, I told my family and teachers I had the flu. One sensei said she was worried that I looked ill. She's very kind and will not fail me even if I'm absent in her class. No sensei will fail me for being sick. The day I graduate, I can wear my graduation kimono. Then I'll announce my news to everyone.

We don't know what our parents will say. I think my family will be more shocked than Naoto's family. My mother will want us to get married straight away, but Naoto said that we can't marry until after I graduate. I agree with him because I want to be a mother who graduated with a college degree, not like my mother who only graduated from high school.

Some people will say that our marriage is *dekichatta-kon;* they will be older because many people of our age have baby-marriage.

I don't know where we will live, probably with Naoto's family. I don't know about the money situation, but our parents will help us. There are so many things that we need to talk about. I never thought this would happen to me, but now I'll be a mother and a wife, and that will be my job. This is a double joy celebration.

Aki

Sixteen-year-old Aki looked confused at my question before launching into a list of her own questions for me.

"When you say that you want to know about where I lived, what do you mean? When I was in elementary school? Because we lived in Hoshigaoka then. Or when we went to Taiwan? Or do you mean the time we came back to Japan when I was in high school? Or do you mean live, as in when we lived with my dad? Or when my parents got divorced, and my mother and I moved to Ikeshita?"

Half of her long hair fell in front of the right side of her face, the other half was held back by a pink clip with a plastic sparkly butterfly perched on top of it. She wore no makeup on her oval-shaped face with its sturdy features; a wide mouth and full lips, a small but broad nose sitting prominently in the middle of her face, while her large dark brown eyes often flickered downwards at the end of most of her comments.

"Wow, you moved a lot," I said a little too strongly, quickly adding, "like me when I was your age," trying to make her feel comfortable.

"Your parents are also divorced?" she asked, looking straight at me. *So much for me making her feel at ease.*

"Err no, but my parents lived apart a lot because of my dad's job. I also lived away from home and moved to different countries while I was going to school... and it wasn't easy."

She smiled and I relaxed.

"No, it's not easy, but it's life." She sounded like an old wise woman.

"Tell me anything you want about where you lived, what places, or with whom, anything."

"Anything? Okay," and she giggled.

"I liked living in Hoshigaoka when I was young. My parents were together, and I liked my school. I had many friends, no one called me names, no bullying, and the teachers were very kind. I think it was the best time of my life in Japan.

But I remember at night after I went to bed, I would hear my mother complaining to my dad, her voice would go on and on, and sometimes she would argue and cry. It was always about money. How she needed money to buy food and get things for the house, for me, for her and him, too. My dad never said anything back. I felt bad for him. No matter what, I think he was, is, a good dad.

During the week, he worked for a company. I don't know what he did, but he would travel overseas sometimes. That's where he met my mother, on a business trip to Taiwan.

On weekends, he would go out a lot, so I didn't see him much. But whenever he came home from work, he always bought me chocolates. He would leave them on the kitchen table if I was already in bed so I could take them to school the next day. I think he did that for maybe 11 years. Not 11, because I would have been a baby, but from kindergarten.

Then when I was about 8 years old, every Friday night, he would buy us Domino's pizza. My mother loved pizza and other foreign food. I did too. We'd all eat pizza together and then watch television. My friends would ask me on Monday if I had pizza on Friday, and they would say I was lucky.

"They thought you were lucky to eat pizza?" I interrupted, not meaning to do so.

"Only my two friends said it. The other students probably thought it was normal because I was foreign. I never felt foreign though, not at that time. I felt Japanese. My mother always told me, "Your father is Japanese, you were born in Japan, you have a Japanese name, you are Japanese." Later she told me something else, but when I was in elementary school, she would always tell me I was Japanese, and I should tell other children that if they teased me.

"I remembered something funny, my mother didn't speak perfect Japanese, but she had learned English in Taiwan, and sometimes when she was angry at my Dad, she would say things in English. He didn't understand, but I did. She would say, "You're stupid" or "You idiot", and if she was really mad, she would say things in Chinese to him."

"What language did she speak to you?" I was always interested in multilingual families and how members of a family would choose the same or different languages to speak to each other.

"Urm, well, she would speak to me in Chinese when we were alone, Japanese when she was around my dad or other people, and then she would speak in English to foreign people. She would also make me read books in English and watch movies in English because she wanted me to know three languages. She told me her dream was for me to go to America and live."

"Did you have any other family in Hoshigaoka?"

"No. My grandmother, my dad's mother lived in Mie. My grandfather died when I was three. My dad is an only child like me. My mother's family is all in Taiwan."

"Did you see your grandmother often?"

"Not really, only at New Year's and Obon, when we went to visit her. My mother told me that my grandmother didn't like her. It was always the same conversation in the car when we returned home from my grandmother.

"Why does your mother have to say those things? Like I don't know anything about Japan. I know everything about Japan. It's because I'm

Chinese. She's typical Japanese and doesn't like anyone foreign. I should ask her why her son didn't marry a Japanese woman then. Because they would have to look after her, that's why. Why don't you tell your mother something, Taro? You should tell her she shouldn't speak to me like that. You don't tell her anything because she gives you money. Huh. You should give me that money instead of taking it to spend it. Aki needs many things for school, and I want to buy some clothes because I want to teach Chinese. The woman at the international center asked if I would teach Chinese there. If I'm going to teach there, I need some nice clothes. Why doesn't your mother buy some clothes and shoes for Aki? You should tell her that her granddaughter needs many things.

"I remember I never liked the trip home because of my mother's arguments, but I didn't understand why she was like that until the last year of junior high school."

"What happened?"

"My mother was fighting with my father more and more about money. I needed some shoes, but my mother said we had no money because she had to pay for the electricity bill. She was teaching part-time at the international center and she would use that money to buy food.

"One Saturday morning, I heard her talking to her mother, my Chinese grandmother, on the telephone.

"Aki and I will come back to Taiwan next month.

"I thought it was for a holiday.

"After that call, my mother explained that she was very unhappy with my father and he did some bad things, but she didn't say what. She only told me that we would pack enough clothes for a long holiday.

"The day of our flight, my father told me, 'Be good for your mother.'

"Then he halfway hugged me and said goodbye. He was never like fathers you see on American television shows, he was very Japanese. On the other hand, my mother was always hugging and kissing me.

"I didn't see my father for a year after that. We went to Taipei, and my mother enrolled me in junior high school. I stayed there for three years. She explained that she wanted me to go to school in Taiwan to become fluent in Chinese and then get an international job in the future."

"Did you enjoy your life there?"

"Yes, I loved Taiwan, love Taiwan. In school, I made lots of friends. It was so different from Japan. Everyone was friendly on my first day in school. They all wanted to know about Japan and asked me to speak in Japanese. I met my Chinese family as well, and they were nice to me. I missed my dad and I missed my friends from elementary school, but after a while, I got used to living in Taiwan. Everything felt... I don't know, more free or open, something like that. Maybe I was freer. It was easy to live there. I can't explain it, people seemed happy and no one cared too much about things. I can't explain it. It wasn't Nagoya."

"How about language?"

"At first, I was really shy because I didn't speak good Chinese. My mother used to speak to me in Mandarin and a kind of dialect, mixed together. I didn't realize this until I came to Taiwan, and then I realized some words she had said were in the Taiwanese dialect and not the proper Mandarin word. My mother got me a private tutor when we arrived, so I had Chinese lessons after school to help me. I remember this one time when this student made fun of me and how I spoke, and everyone got angry with him. They supported me. They said I was learning, and it was difficult for me.

"We also studied English in school, and it was different from

Japanese. We had foreign teachers, and everyone wanted to speak in English. We watched English television and movies, and sung songs in English. My English was very good when I left Taiwan. Of course, my Chinese was too, and I didn't forget Japanese. In my last year of junior high school, my mother got a Japanese tutor for me. She said she was thinking of going back to Japan, especially for my high school education. She wanted me to go to university in Japan. "My mother got her old job back in Taipei teaching Japanese to Taiwanese businesspeople; it was how she met my dad through a student who was employed by a Japanese company. One of her student's had a Japanese wife, I don't know why he had to take classes in Japanese, but his wife was the one who gave me Japanese lessons after school."

"Did you feel that your identity was still Japanese?"

"No. I can say because I lived in Taiwan, I felt more Taiwanese. All the customs and festivals that my mother had told me about when I was in Japan, I got to take part in them with my family, so it made me feel more like this was my culture.

"In school and in my family, everyone treated me like Taiwanese, even though I was born in Japan, could speak Japanese, had a Japanese name and a Japanese father; no one said, 'You're Japanese or you're foreign.' Everyone said, 'You are still Taiwanese,' or sometimes 'You're mixed Taiwanese,' or 'international Taiwanese.' My mother also started to say that I was mixed Taiwanese and, "It's good to be from two cultures."

"I had two friends, one who was older than me, and one who was in my class, who were also mixed Taiwanese. Amy, who was in my class, was born in Taipei, but her father was from Canada. It was funny to go to her house and hear her father and everyone speaking in Mandarin. My other friend, Juita, was in the class higher than me, and she was Taiwanese and

Malaysian. She was the head of the English club at our school. She was so kind when I left junior high."

"What happened?" I asked.

"My mother decided that we should go back to Japan, and I saw Juita the day my mother told me. Juita hugged me and said she knew how hard it was to keep moving to and from Taiwan, and that I should email or call her if I felt sad or homesick."

"That was nice. And how many times had you seen your father by then?" I was interested in how she viewed her relationship with him.

"I saw him once a year. He also sent a few emails and we spoke on the phone, maybe three or four times a year."

"How did you feel about that and going back to Japan?" I asked hesitantly, knowing I had asked a double question.

Aki shrugged her shoulders slightly before answering with a dry,

"Okay."

"Okay about contact with your dad, or okay about going back to Japan?"

"I was happy when I saw my dad. He bought me gifts and Japanese sweets that I couldn't get in Taipei. I only saw him for a day every year because he was on a business trip. I was happy but, how to say this, I was happy that I lived in Taipei, so I wasn't unhappy. When he left the first time, he said he would visit once a year and he kept his promise."

"And emails and phone calls?" I prompted.

"He asked the same things, how was school and what club I was in? That's all. He's very Japanese. Oh, he also sent gifts for my birthday and New Year's, Japanese New Year not Chinese New Year. Another thing, when he came to Taiwan, we always went for pizza. That was nice. He was getting so fat though, and every time he came to Taiwan, his hair would be more silver. My mother always spoke to him very nicely and she also came with us for pizza. When he was leaving, she would always give him this package with food and men's clothes, like a present, I think. I asked her once if they were going to divorce and she said she didn't know.

"When we returned to Japan, it was very hard for us. Actually, it was a shock. My father wasn't home when we arrived from the airport, he was at work.

"We arrived at our *aparto* in Hoshigaoka, and it was so dirty, like no one had cleaned for years. But that was not the only shock. The apartment was nearly empty. There was no television, no computer, no CD player, nothing, just a *kotatsu*, and a sofa. I was ashamed that was how my father lived. My mother started to cry and said that we should go back to Taipei. I remembered there was no kettle, so my mother boiled some water in a big old pan, and she washed two cups and we sat on the floor and drank tea. Then my mother told me the truth.

"The reason we went to Taiwan was that Taro used to gamble, not just *pachinko* but other things as well, I don't know what. But he had to take out loans to pay the rent and bills because he had no money. Even though he had a job, he had to give all his money to the company that gave him the loan. I found this out little by little.

"When I met him in Taiwan, he said he had an apartment, a good job, he was the only son and he would inherit his parents' house; he made it sound like he was wealthy. When I came to Japan, I saw he was only a *sararīman*, but it wasn't so bad because I liked Japan and then I had you. Soon, I realized that he had less and less money.

"When we left, it was because he told me he had no money for the next month's rent. I was afraid for us, so that's why we went to Taiwan.

"When I wrote to your father and told him we were going to come back to Japan, he said that's good. Now I think I made a mistake."

"When my father came home that evening, my mother argued with him and said she wanted a divorce if he was still gambling. But he said he had stopped. He said the loan company had taken the television and computer because he hadn't paid for one or two months, but that was a while ago. He said to my mother that she should stay in Japan, and so we did for a year. But there were no more chocolates or sweets for me when he returned home from work, and we never again had pizza on Friday like we used to.

"My first year in high school, I hated it. I was excited at first to go because I thought it would be like my elementary school, but it wasn't. No one talked to me. They called me Chinese. The teacher introduced me to the class and said I had come from Taiwan, and everyone should make me welcome, but they didn't.

"Only two girls, Michiko and Eiko, were nice to me and asked where I was from and why I was in Japan. When I told them I was born in Japan and my father was Japanese, they were shocked. I didn't know why. They said my Japanese was really good and they're my friends now, but it's not like my friends in Taipei.

"The other students called me names, and in the corridor, sometimes, they would push me and then say '*gomen*', but they would be laughing. I hated, hate them. I had stomach aches every morning for that first year and when I saw the school gates, I wanted to vomit.

"Sometimes in class, if we were talking about Asian countries or culture, the teacher would ask me, 'Aki chan, tell us about Taiwan, how are Taiwanese people or culture or something like that.' I didn't know what to say because I didn't want to speak to anyone. Students would laugh if I stayed silent, but if I talked or said something quietly, they would tease me after class.

"'Chinese people are stupid and ugly.' I heard that all the time.

"When students found out that I was *ha-fu*, that made it worse.

"'You are half, you're not whole. You only have half a brain, you only speak half Japanese.'

"Finally, I told my mother that I was being teased at school and she went to the principal. I told her not to go, but she said she wanted to let him know the situation. But when she came back from his office, she was so angry, and she told my father.

"Japanese people are so stupid. The principal told me if Aki has a problem with the students, maybe I should move her to another school. Why should I move her? Why doesn't he stop the students from attacking our daughter? What attitude is that? It's not Aki's fault, she's not the problem. Japan is so backward."

"My father agreed with the principal's view, which made my mother angrier. He thought it would be better for me not to face that kind of treatment. But even if I could move, there was nowhere to move me because this was the nearest high school to where I lived, and we were halfway through the school year. I had to stay for the whole year and put up with it. I didn't tell my mother everything after that; I didn't tell anyone some of the things those students told me.

"I remember one night, I saw this television program where foreigners spoke about their experiences living in Japan, and they said Japanese people are prejudiced. I thought so, too. I also saw this interview with a girl who was like me, half Japanese and half American, but she had many friends in school. I think it's different if you're half-American or your parent is from one of those countries like Canada or Australia. If you're half Chinese, no one thinks about you in this way, you are not *ha-fu*, you're nothing."

She stopped to take a sip of her tea, now cold, and I had an opportunity to speak.

"Aki, you know I'm mixed too, and although I didn't experience some of those things, I know what it's like to feel as if you don't have a place. For example, look at my face; do you see any Chinese in it?"

She laughed.

"But my Haka heritage is still there, seen or unseen. People always think they know our identity from what we look like, or where our parents are from, and you and I know it's not as simple as that." I considered out loud, thinking about the identity issues I had faced growing up.

Looking back at Aki, I gently added, "You had a really hard year, Aki chan, but you got through it; that shows real strength."

"Yes, it was hard. My mother got a job teaching Chinese in a private company, and she told me she was going to try and save her money so we could move again because she thought my father was still gambling.

"We had very little money. My mother bought a television from the recycle shop; we would buy most of our things for the home there. Sometimes my mother would look near our apartment building when it was the big *gomi* day for furniture and other things. If she saw something good, she and I would go at night when we thought people couldn't see us and get whatever it was. In Japan, people throw away some good things.

"Our main shopping place was the recycle shop though, they had everything. I got a jacket there, and my mother would get most of her clothes there. I can tell you these things because you're foreign and foreign people have a different attitude about recycled things. But I can never tell anyone else.

"By the end of my first year in high school, my mother told me she was going to divorce my father, so we went to look at apartments secretly. I was happy. It was hard to live with my father. He smoked all the time when he came home, and he also drank beer. He smelled. The main thing was we didn't have money, and my mother said he wasn't paying the bills again, so he would probably get another loan.

"My mother and father never slept in the same bedroom. She and I slept in one bedroom together on the same futon and my father slept in the other bedroom. When we found a 1LDK in Ikeshita for 45,000 yen, which my mother said was very cheap, she and I also slept in the same bedroom and shared a futon. "The day we moved to Ikeshita, my father was at work and I was at school. My mother moved our things into it with the help of her foreign friend, an American man called Dan. He worked for Toyota and had a car, so he moved our suitcases for us. My mother met Dan at the company where she taught Chinese. He was learning Japanese and she said she would give him free lessons on Saturday morning at his house in Gokiso.

"'If I divorce your father, maybe I can marry someone like Dan, then you can go to America to study.'

"My mother told me that she wanted Dan to be her boyfriend, but he only wanted to be friends. I didn't mind if my mother re-married again. I could never marry anyone like my dad. I like my dad and he's a good dad, but I don't want a husband like him.

"When we moved to Ikeshita, we didn't have many things in our apartment, but at least it was clean. My mother got a second job, and she seemed happier because she could organize her money better and knew what bills we would have to pay.

"I enrolled in another school nearer to me. I told my mother not to tell the new school that we had come from Taiwan a year ago, only that we had moved from Hoshigaoka. They would know she was Chinese, but I thought it would be better if I was a mostly Japanese girl who had come from another school.

"Although I was new at the school, it was a little better. I decided to keep myself separate, stay by myself. If someone came up to me and talked, then I would talk back, otherwise, I would stay alone. I think it's better to be like this when you are new or foreign or just different. You'll still get called names, but I think it's not as bad. I didn't get teased until I had English class.

"Japanese English classes are boring and stupid. In my school in Taipei, English was our favorite subject, and everyone wanted to learn it. In Japan, it is the opposite. I always got an A in my homework for English, as it was easy. When we had to read aloud, I would read in the Japanese way, do you know what I mean? It sounds so stupid, but I did it anyway.

"However, then we got this new foreign teacher from New Zealand. Her name was Jennifer. She encouraged all the students to talk in English, and sometimes I forgot and spoke in the way I had learned in Taiwan like an American, not the Japanese way. I would see some students looking at me, and then I'd realize what I was saying and go back to speaking the Japanese way.

"Jennifer gave us homework to write about another culture, so I chose Taiwan because it was easy for me. About a week later, she asked me to read my homework aloud in class. I read it aloud in the Japanese way.

"Then she asked me how I knew so much about Taiwan and I didn't know what to say. I couldn't lie because maybe someone would find out I was half-Taiwanese because they had seen my mother. So I had to say my mother was from Taiwan, but she'd lived in Japan for many years. Then everyone said, 'Really? You are *ha-fu*?'

"After class, Jennifer called me aside and asked if I had studied English outside of school, and I told her I'd had some lessons. She said, 'I get the feeling that you know a lot of English, your work is very good. But in class, you don't always say that you know the answers. You need to speak up more. It will help the other students.'

"She didn't understand that I had no intention of helping anyone. After I spoke to her, I then had to explain to these three girls standing by my locker that although I was *ha-fu*, I was more Japanese because I didn't know much about Taiwan. They asked if I had ever gone to Taiwan and if I liked it. I said I had gone on holiday, but I didn't like it. Then the teasing started again.

"'You are strange, you are weird because you're only half.'

"'Don't talk to the *ha-fu*.'

"'She looks more like ugly Chinese.'

"I didn't care so much then what anybody said as the teasing wasn't as bad as my last school, and I only had a year and a half before I graduated from high school."

"Tell me something, Aki. You talked about your identity before. How would you describe yourself now?" I asked.

"Hmm, it depends. My mother still says I'm mixed, and it is good that I have two cultures. I feel I am mixed inside my head. But I think if I am in Japan, it's not good to be mixed. Either I have to say I am full Japanese or foreign. I can't say I'm full Japanese, because if anyone meets my mother, then they'll know I am not. If my mother didn't live here, then maybe I would say I was Japanese. But right now, I don't want to say I'm Japanese. I don't like how Japanese people are, I prefer to be Taiwanese. To be honest, sometimes inside my heart, I wish I were full Taiwanese. I like the culture of Taiwan, I liked my life in Taipei, the way my family was, they were very warm. I felt it was easier to be anything I wanted to be in Taiwan.

"In Japan, everyone is put into boxes, and I cannot fit into a Japanese box. That's not my fault. It's because my mother and father got married, and now they're divorced, so I am not only *ha-fu* in my culture, I am *ha-fu* in my family, too. I don't understand why Japanese people can't accept that not everyone is the same, not every family is the same. I'm born in Japan, but I'm not made in Japan. I don't know how else to explain my life."

Yuri

"I don't know who I prefer. It's difficult to answer this question, but I think it's better to be with a Japanese because we know how to be in our society; we can understand each other's minds easier. I dated two foreign girls, and to be honest, it was easy to be with them. Foreign girls are free, but still, we also had some problems because," Yuri paused, knowing she needed to finish her sentence diplomatically to the foreign woman sitting opposite to her. "It's not their fault," she concluded, "they didn't live here a long time and they don't understand Japanese culture. Our culture is not easy to learn."

Initially, she had jumped at the opportunity to be interviewed by twenty-four-year-old Theresa, an American English teacher writing an article on lesbian experiences in Japan. She harbored playful thoughts that she might end up dating her as they were the same age. Perhaps she would be introduced to some other attractive foreign women, but upon meeting Theresa, she knew neither was a possibility. Theresa was definitely not her type; too tall, too unfashionable in her baggy jeans and creased t-shirt, and although Yuri liked the eagle tattoo Theresa had on her upper arm, this American girl looked too much like a man, too *tachi.* In her opinion, foreign lesbians were rarely *neko*.

"What do you mean foreign women don't understand Japanese culture? Can you explain it?" Theresa asked seriously, tapping her pen gently on the notepad before writing what seemed to be one word.

"Hmm, it's difficult. I think foreign women, lesbians, are very free, they're very open. I think in America or Europe countries, it is easy to be gay or lesbian. Here in Japan, it is not so easy, and we Japanese have ways, even among lesbians, we have ways." She couldn't explain it but was compelled to go on, as Theresa looked at her with a fixed stare. "How to say this . . . when you meet someone in Japan, among lesbians, it's normal to say what you are."

"What do you mean? Do you mean like *neko* or *tachi or...*?" Theresa asked.

"*Sou sou*, yes, yes." Yuri was relieved that she wouldn't have to explain this to the journalist. "The club you went to, 'Crush', did you wear a bracelet?"

"No, the women at the entrance said it was okay not to wear one. I don't like the idea of having to choose something like that. It was weird to do that. I didn't see this at Maxim when I was there."

"Yes, Maxim has more foreigners in it, but in other Japanese lesbian bars, you'll find bracelets or sometimes necklaces, something to let everyone know. I think we do this only in Japan, and it's one example of a problem I had with my ex-girlfriend, Louise. She was from California, an American, and she always got angry if we went to a bar and she saw those bracelets. She'd try to argue with the people there about why they had these bracelets. To be honest, sometimes I felt embarrassed. A manager once said to me I should explain to my foreign friend that she was in Japan and this is our way. I tried many times to tell her that it made it easy for us to know what kind of lesbian you were and who you were looking for. So if you were more boyish, masculine or dominant, then you took the *boi or tachi* bracelet, as you saw in Crush, or if you were more feminine, then you took the *femme* or *neko* one, or if they had the *ri-be* one..."

"Sorry what? *Ri-be*?" Theresa looked confused.

"Yes, *ri-be*, it is short for *riberaru*, freedom for both, liberal, sometimes you are *neko*, sometimes *tachi*."

"Wow, I didn't know that one. Liberal can mean something different in the US," and she smiled broadly at Yuri, who didn't understand the connotation.

"For we Japanese, it makes it easier to know who you are and what you want when you go to a club. But Louise always got angry and said it was very Japanese to be so inflexible about what role you played and who you liked. But to me, it made sense. Why am I going to waste my time talking to a girl, only to then find out that she's not interested in me? It is better to identify yourself in the beginning. It's more considerate this way. You're thinking of the other person. You don't waste someone's time and they don't waste yours."

"But are you fixed in what kind of woman you are and what kind of woman you want as a partner throughout your whole life? That's a bit strange. Isn't it better to be, err, *ri-be*? Then you have a choice. I understand what you're saying about letting someone know what you like but...."

She's just like Louise; all these foreign women were.

"Louise said those things too. But I think you don't go from one way to another. You are either one or the other." Yuri was aware that her voice sounded more firm and deeper when she said this because she knew she was right. No matter how much Louise had argued with her about this issue, the fact was Louise was *femme-neko*, just as she was *boi-tachi* and that would never change.

"So what bracelet do you take? If that's not too personal."

"I take the *tachi* bracelet," Yuri responded flatly.

"Really? I thought you might be more *femme-neko*."

This annoyed Yuri. It was obvious to most girls in the bars, with or without a bracelet, that she was *tachi*. "Why? Do I look like *neko* to you?" she replied, more irritated. The interview was not going the way she had originally envisaged.

"Well, to be honest, if you were in the US, you'd probably be considered more *femme* because of how you dress and your hairstyle. It's kind of cute. I mean it looks boyish, but it's a kind of cute, feminine boyish. Shit, I can't stand talking in these terms. It's so rigid."

Yes, she was so much like Louise.

"I guess I would be considered *tachi*, right?" she continued, nodding her head in agreement at Yuri as if Yuri had already answered.

"Yes, in Japan, you're very *tachi*."

"But just to return, you really don't think people can change what kind of woman they like over time?"

"Have you changed who you are?" Yuri snapped back. "Maybe in America, lesbians change from one way to another, but not in Japan. Most lesbians here know who they are and what they like."

"Hmm, that's a great statement for the article which I'm sure will bring a lot of comments. Okay, can I ask you this? Can you tell me how you see your future? I mean as a lesbian. Do you see yourself with a life partner? Would you like to get married? Or have children?"

Yuri paused for a minute, trying to gather her thoughts about marriage. She was very definite in her view about marrying another woman.

"Everyone wants love and to be with someone. I don't believe in getting married. I think that's for straight people. I see gay couples in other countries getting married, but I'm not interested in doing that, it seems wrong. Also, in Japan, it'd be difficult to live with another woman as a couple, people might say something. For me, I'd think about my family. I don't want them to have to explain to anyone about my life. It'd be too difficult for them. They know I don't want to get married and they accept it; I don't want to make it harder for them. I think it is better for me to live alone and have a girlfriend who lives somewhere else. As for children, I don't want any."

"Interesting," Theresa mused and then wrote in her notebook for a second or two. Yuri lifted her head slightly so she could read the words on the pad. She saw 'society' and 'family' in their upside-down position.

"So you're worried about how it would look if you lived with another woman, you said it was wrong?"

"Maybe not wrong, although to me it seems strange. I don't know, these issues are new to Japan. I'm not worried, but I'd consider my family. I can't speak for every lesbian, but for me and my friends, our aim is to live independently, on our own, have a job, have girlfriends, be able to travel, have fun, and be free. Getting married and having children sounds too traditional. Why are you going to run to something that you are running from? Marriage is something we want to get away from."

"Okay, so are you politically active?"

These questions were definitely from a western woman. Who cares about politics in Japan? Politics equals a bunch of old men.

"I don't care about politics," she said flatly.

"What I mean is," Louise insisted, "are you active in LGBT rights, do you go on pride marches, things like that?"

"No, I haven't gone on any marches here. Maybe I would if I were in another city and my friends were going, but not here because of my family. I don't want to embarrass them because the march might be on these streets or television, and they might see me, or someone they know could see me."

"Do you wish that your family would know that you're a lesbian? Do you think it would be nice to bring a girlfriend home?"

"I don't think about that. I don't see why it's important to tell them that I'm lesbian. Maybe they know already, but they'll never say, and I won't say either. The way things are now is fine for both of us. I go home for New Year's and other family events. I told my mother when I was in college that I'd never get married, and she said it was okay as long as I was happy. My father never really said anything. My sister is married with a child, so I think they're happy with that. If I had a girlfriend, I might bring her home, but I wouldn't say, 'This is my lesbian girlfriend.' My girlfriend, if she is Japanese, would also be the same as me. There's no need to say everything in the open. Personal lives are private, and in Japan, there's respect for this." Yuri hoped that Theresa would understand this point because Louise never did.

"Do you think there's any discrimination against lesbians in Japan?" Theresa continued.

"I think if you're open about it, people might say some things. Some people discriminate against gay men, but I don't know about lesbians."

"So you think you shouldn't be open about your sexual identity?" *She really didn't understand the idea of privacy in Japan.*

"It depends. Some people in our generation don't care what you are, so if they ask, you can just say 'I'm lesbian.' But the older generation doesn't understand and the family might find it difficult, so I think you shouldn't say any of these things. I know in other countries, everyone wants to be open, but in Japan, we have to consider our families and the society. I work in a shoe shop and my salary is enough for me to live alone and pay my bills. I don't have a lot of money but it's okay because I'm independent. I live for the weekends when I can go to the bar and drink, dance, and have fun, and maybe meet a cute girl."

"So you're happy with your life?"

"Yes. If I stay like this for the next 40 or 50 years, I would say I have a good life."

"A good life as a lesbian in Japan?"

"That's a strange question. If I say I have a good life, does it matter if I am lesbian or I'm in Japan? Maybe this is the problem for foreign lesbians, they can't imagine that to be a Japanese lesbian can equal to having a good life. Perhaps now I understand for myself why it's easier for me to date Japanese women."

Mami

"But I don't know what to tell you, my life is so ... it's so normal. There's nothing special about me. I'm an ordinary Japanese girl who works."

Mami giggled slightly. Her smile was a permanent fixture on her face, but it wasn't false. That smile that had helped everyone from classmates with their homework, to parents and a sibling with regular gifts, was now extended to passengers and their queries on the *Linimo*, the electric monorail that took commuters nine stops to and from the city limits to the semi-rural areas of Nagoya.

"Let me put these away and then I'll sign out. I'll meet you upstairs in *Mister Donuts.*"

In her right hand was a miniature small broom with its connected dustpan; mandatory tools for being a platform attendant. In addition to assisting the passengers with information, watching them get on and off the train, guiding them into a less crowded carriage during rush hours, checking that they or their items were not stuck in a closing door, signaling to a supervisor that it was safe for the driver-less monorail to depart the station, platform attendants working at this final destination station also had to clean the *Linimo* carriages before they departed.

"What shall I tell you? I don't know," she asked and answered, shrugging her shoulders, which simultaneously raised her stiff navy-blue military-styled jacket with its gleaming gold buttons. Her spotless uniform was too big for her small frame. Sitting down at the table with two cinnamon donuts and a cup of hot coffee, her straight skirt falling to below her knees looked as if it could comfortably spin around her body.

"Tell me about your work, anything you like. Do you like your job?" I asked.

"Urm," she giggled. "I like it. Sometimes, I think." Her head bent and eyes momentarily looked down at her donuts before she faced me again with a smile, "No, I do like it. I'm very fortunate to have gotten this job.

"In my class, Kako and I were the only two who got full-time jobs with good companies. Kako works at the airport for ANA. Sayako, Ayumi, and Eriko got full-time positions at their *arubeito,* and I think Etsuko and Kaori are working for fashion shops, not big *departos,* but smaller places. Misaki and Rika are working in a kindergarten; Natsuko and Rie, I'm not sure, maybe they are still at their *arubeito*.

"I was very lucky, but I applied very early for this job. At the end of my first year of junior college, I went to the *Linimo* office and asked how it was possible to apply there. The manager gave me all the information. I remember he said he was impressed because I was brave to come to the office by myself and ask him about a job. I didn't think I was brave because I knew it was difficult to get a job, so I had no choice. Maybe no choice makes you brave.

"I remember I was sitting on the *Linimo* coming from college and I was thinking about my future. I wanted to work for JR or one of the big train companies. But I thought that those places would only hire four-year university students and not someone like me with a junior college degree. Also, my parents were not very wealthy, but they sent me to this college, which was expensive for them because they heard that if you graduate from here you can get a job, but I know that's not true.

"Four-year students can't find jobs, and so students like me, especially girl students, it's difficult, very difficult, and the college didn't help us find jobs. They encouraged us and gave us training in many things, like how to talk at an interview with a good, kind voice, how to be polite and use polite language with our co-workers and bosses. We also had two guest speakers, ladies from local companies who told us about their jobs, but the college didn't introduce us to any companies and get us interviews like my parents thought they would. Maybe they did that in the four-year university, but not for us.

"My mother was very worried about my job situation when I was in college. My parents didn't have money for me to transfer to the four-year university because I have a sister who's two years younger than me. She's now at college and my parents have to pay for her to go to a college as they did with me.

"I felt very bad that my mother was trying to find a way for me to transfer to a four-year university if I didn't get a job. She said she would try and work more hours at the supermarket. My father works in an electric company, he works on machinery, I don't know what he does, but he works very long hours. I felt guilty about their situation, so I knew I had to find a job somewhere.

"Also, I had another reason for wanting to find a job. I wanted to stay in Nagoya. My family is from Toyama, which is far away, and where they live is in the countryside. I love Nagoya, it's a big city and fun to live here.

"When I was at college, my parents paid for a small *mansion* for me. It cost 45,000 *yen,* and they paid for the electric and telephone bill. The water bill was in my rent. I worked at Circle K to pay for everything else I needed.

"It was so exciting to live on my own in the beginning. I had to cook for myself, wash my own clothes, do everything for myself. When I was in high school, my mother used to wake me up in the morning; she made all our meals, washed our clothes, bought our clothes, everything. Now I had to rely on my alarm clock to wake up, do all the housework myself, and even work out my money by myself. I really appreciate my mother whenever I think that she did all that work, and she also worked at the *supa*.

"But living alone was being free. I could do whatever I wanted in my own apartment and I think I became very independent. My friends and I used to talk about how happy we were that we lived alone for that feeling of freedom.

"But at the same time, it was lonely. You come home to silence. Only me and the television. Now I pay for internet so I can chat online, but still, when I come home, it's silent, I'm silent. I don't use my voice unless I come to work or go to the *supa*.

"Still, I prefer to live with loneliness than to live with my family in Toyama. Does that sound bad? I love my family, but I love my life here. I think that is what made me brave to find out information for this job.

"I filled out the application and went through the interview process. There were lots of young people like me. The woman who interviewed me was very nice. She explained everything that I had to do. There was a man there as well, but he didn't say much.

"When I received the letter that I had been successful, I called my mother first. She was so happy. My father was too and my sister. They couldn't believe I did it all on my own.

"Working for the *Linimo* is a career job, if you stay a long time with the company, you get lots of benefits. Right now, I'm a platform attendant, but I can work my way up and get promotion.

"I'm so lucky to have this job because I was able to move and get another *mansion* for about the same rent, but nearer to my work. I pay for everything myself. My mother always asks me if I need anything and I tell her

I'm fine. To be honest, I don't have a lot of money left after I pay rent, bills, and other things, but it's okay. I feel proud I can do this for myself at my age. Maybe when I get to twenty-five-years-old, I will be able to save some money and go on vacation by myself. But right now, I can't save anything.

"After work, I go to the *combini* next to my apartment building. When that 7-11 opened, I was happy as I could eat most of my meals from there. It's so easy to microwave meals and not have to cook. But my favorite meals are from McDonald's or KFC. I can choose which one I like because both are near to my house.

"The McDonald's is very big and has lots of seats for single people. I really like this idea. When I was in high school, the McDonald's near our school only had a few seats for single people. Sometimes one person would sit at a table for two or four, and everyone had to wait or take out their meal. But this new McDonald's has most of its seats for single people, and at each of the tables, there is a place to plug in your phone or laptop. It's so good. Sometimes I sit there for two hours on a Friday after work. I get a set McDonald's meal and I can play games on my phone or text friends. It's fun!

"The KFC is quieter, so I go there when McDonald's is busy, but they do not have the connection for laptops and phones. I make sure my battery is fully charged before I go there.

"The other thing I do after work is to go window shopping. I don't have a lot of money to buy clothes, but I love to look at clothes and imagine what it would be like to wear them. I walk through the underground mall or go to the *shotengais* and look at everything. I usually go by myself. If my friends have time on the weekend, then we can meet and shop, but it isn't often. The last time was six months ago.

"Sayako introduced me to this computer program where you can put your photo in and then try on different outfits. I love that program and spend hours on it. Sometimes I spend my whole Saturday on my *pascom* trying on different outfits. I'd love to find a program where I can put a photo of my face in and change my hair or make-up. I think there is a program like that, I need to find it. But that's what I do most of my time off, go online and look for things to do.

"Friends? I keep in contact with Sayako the most, but also Kako, Misaki, Ayumi, and Eriko, all my college friends. We try to meet for dinner every six months or longer, but we text each other more.

"I don't really have friends at work. Everyone is very kind and helpful, they are office friends, but not like my college friends. I am the youngest in the office. There is no one my age, no girl or boy, everyone else is much older, and some are as old as my parents with grown-up children.

"For me, when I went to school and college, those were my days for friendship. I treasure my friends from that time. I remember my father told me a long time ago, "always remember your school friends because when you start to work, you never have true friends."

"I'd like to have a boyfriend, but I don't know where to meet him. I sometimes wonder how I'll get married, because there's no one at work and I don't know anyone else. That part of my life is difficult.

"A long time ago, it was easier to meet a husband. My mother and father met in high school. On graduation day, my father told my mother that he liked her, but my mother said she didn't like him because he wasn't so nice-looking.

"My father got a job at the electric company where he still works, and my mother worked at a dental office. About three years after their graduation, my father came into the dental office because he had a toothache. When my mother saw him, she said he looked more mature. He asked to meet her again and she said yes; very soon after they got married.

"It seemed so easy when she talked about it to my sister and me.

"'Your father had a good job and he wanted to marry me. I didn't think too much about how he looked then because I wanted to get married and have children. Our families were very happy about our marriage and they helped us to get our house. I was able to quit my job after a year of marriage, and then you, Mami, were born and two years later, you, Midori. Nowadays, everything is changing so quickly, and I think girls want too much from boys.'

"My mother says that our generation wants boys to be good-looking and rich or we won't marry them, but it's not true. She thinks that's the reason I don't have a boyfriend, but it isn't. I don't know where to find a boyfriend.

"Sometimes if I go out with my friends, we see nice boys, but they don't come and talk to us, I don't know why. They want girls who are very pretty and slim. I'm not that pretty and I've put on weight, I'm 47 kilos now, I used to be 44 in college. I need to go on a diet.

"I don't know what my future will be, whether I'll get married or not, or whether I'll even find a boyfriend, but I'm glad I have a job. That's the most important thing for me right now. I know that I spend a lot of time alone, but it's okay, I don't think I'm the only one. I have my family that I visit once a year. I have friends that I see every few months. I also have internet so I can do things at home by myself, like look at clothes.

"If I'm the same way without a boyfriend or a husband in ten years, I think I might get a pet, a cat or a dog. Ayumi has a cat and she says it's her best friend. I'm seriously thinking about whether I should also get a pet, although it means that I won't be able to go on vacation, if I ever go on vacation.

"So this is my life. I told you it's normal, nothing special. I'm like all other Japanese girls who work; I'm lucky to have this life.

Glossary

aparto	apartment
arubaito	part-time job
boi	boy
chan	a diminutive suffix expressing that the speaker finds a person endearing, used for babies, young children, and teenagers, close female friends
combini	convenience store
daikon	white radish
Daiso	name of a popular Japanese store selling merchandise for 100 yen or more
dekichatta-kon	phrase for marriage resulting from pregnancy/pre-marital pregnancy
genkan	traditional Japanese entryway areas for a house, apartment, or building, a combination of a porch and a doormat
gomen	I'm sorry
gomi	garbage/trash/rubbish
ha-fu	Half, in this case referring to a person of mixed Japanese heritage
ichi man yen	10,000 yen (Japanese currency)
ikebana	Japanese art of flower arrangement

kawaii	lovable, cute, adorable
Kawaramachi dori	name of a popular main shopping street in Kyoto
kotatsu	a low, wooden table frame covered by a futon, or heavy blanket, upon which a tabletop sits, underneath is a heat source usually electric
kowai	scared, afraid, scary or I'm scared
mansion	a micro-apartment, one room apartment
meishi	business card
metabo	overweight, fat
neko	cat
onee san	older sister, big sister
pachinko	recreational arcade game, frequently used as a gambling device
pascom	personal computer
rezubian	lesbian
riberaru	liberal
rokku	rock
sararīmen	salaryman – a man whose income is salary based, particularly males who work for companies and corporations

Seijin No Hi	Coming of Age Day, a Japanese holiday held annually in January to congratulate all those who have reached the age of legal majority (20 years old) over the past year
sempai	used to address or refer to one's senior colleagues in a school, dojo, or sports club; the students in higher grades than oneself are sempai.
shakai-jin	to be an adult member of society
shotengai (s)	a style of Japanese shopping district running along a certain street
soupurando	Soapland - part of Japan's sex industry based on non-penetrative sex between prostitutes and clients
supa	supermarket
tachi	Masculine, 'butch'
takoyaki	a ball-shaped Japanese snack made of a batter filled with minced or diced octopus (*tako*) cooked in a special pan
Totoro	character from the animated movie *"My neighbor Totoro/Tonari no Totoro"*
yakitori	a Japanese type of skewered chicken, grilled

About the author

Marina Mia Cunin is a Social-Anthropologist who has lived and worked in Japan for significant periods of time from 1994-2012. She has twenty years of research and university teaching experience in the UK, Japan, Trinidad and Tobago, and the USA, in Sociology, Anthropology, and Women's Studies. Her publications including her book "Student Views in Japan" (2004) based on her doctoral research, have concerned higher education systems and the student perspective. She also has published research which focuses on the international student experience, as well as on migration issues.

Printed in Great Britain
by Amazon